TOWER FROM THE NORTH WEST.

A

HISTORY

OF THE

CEMETERY OF MOUNT AUBURN.

BY JACOB BIGELOW,

PRESIDENT OF THE CORPORATION.

———

" But bear me gently forth,
  Beneath the open sky,
Where on the pleasant earth
  'Till night the sunbeams lie.

Leave, at my side, a space
  Where thou shalt come at last
To find a resting place
  When years and griefs are past."

BRYANT.

———

BOSTON AND CAMBRIDGE:

JAMES MUNROE AND COMPANY.

M DCCC LX.

PREFACE.

—◆—

HAVING been a witness and an agent in most of the movements which have taken place in regard to Mount Auburn Cemetery from its commencement to the present time, I have felt it a duty to leave on record some account of the more noticeable occurrences connected with the inception, progress, and management of the first enterprise of its kind in the United States. That this task might be discharged with fidelity, I have strengthened my own reminiscences by those of my friends, as well as by a perusal of the Records of the Corporation, from which frequent extracts are made, and also of such contemporaneous publications and documents as I have, for my own satisfaction, from time to time, preserved.

Thirty years ago, the citizens of this metropolis buried their deceased friends in frequented parts of the city, crowding to the utmost capacity the spaces provided for them, and filling with sepulchres the cellars of their most central churches. So rooted was the attachment to this objectionable, but inveterate custom, that a change of place from the city to the country was not effected without difficulty, and not until after some years of unsuccessful effort on the part of its advocates, and even then only by a fortunate, and as it were, accidental concurrence of circumstances. But the successful experiment of Mount Auburn had no sooner been made, than it was rapidly imitated in all parts of the United States. The attractive and consoling association of the garden with the grave has found a response in almost every considerable city and village of our country. Men seem to have discovered, as it were, a new solace, and almost a new pleasure, in building and decorating their own tombs.*

To the memory of Joseph Story, George W. Brimmer, George Bond, H. A. S. Dearborn, and B. A. Gould, and to my surviving friends and early colleagues, Charles P. Curtis and James Read, this little volume, the token of much pleasant intercourse and grateful remembrance, is now dedicated.

* Mount Auburn was consecrated as a Cemetery in 1831; Laurel Hill, near Philadelphia, was incorporated in 1836; Greenwood Cemetery, near New York, in 1837.

J. B.

CONTENTS.

———◆———

PART I.

PART II.

APPENDIX.

ILLUSTRATIONS.

PART I.

—◆—

HISTORY OF MOUNT AUBURN.

HISTORY

OF

MOUNT AUBURN CEMETERY.

———◆———

ABOUT the year 1825 my attention was drawn
to some gross abuses in the rites of sepulture as
they then existed under churches and in other
receptacles of the dead in the city of Boston. At
the same time, a love of the country, cherished by
the character of my earlier pursuits, had long led
me to desire the institution of a suburban cemetery, in which the beauties of nature should, as
far as possible, relieve from their repulsive features
the tenements of the deceased ; and in which, at
the same time, some consolation to survivors might
be sought in gratifying, as far as possible, the last
social and kindred instincts of our nature.

With these views I requested, in that year, a
meeting of a few gentlemen at my house in
Summer Street, to see what measures might be

thought desirable and practicable for promoting an object of such a character. This original meeting was attended by Messrs. John Lowell, William Sturgis, George Bond, Thomas W. Ward, John Tappan, Samuel P. Gardiner, Nathan Hale, and Jacob Bigelow. Other gentlemen invited expressed their concurrence in the design, but did not attend the meeting. A plan for a cemetery, corresponding to what Mount Auburn now is, composed of family burial lots, separated and interspersed with trees, shrubs, and flowers, in a wood or landscape garden, was submitted by me, and received with approval by the persons present. A committee, consisting of Messrs. Bond and Tappan, was appointed, to look out for a tract of ground suitable for the desired purpose, and the meeting was dissolved. This committee fixed their attention on an estate in Brookline, which afterwards proved to be unattainable, and here the subject rested, without definitive action, for several years.

In the meantime the enterprise, although delayed, was not abandoned. Inquiries continued to be made, and negotiations attempted for various tracts of land advantageously situated in the neighborhood of Boston. Overtures were twice made by me to Mr. Augustus Aspinwall for the then beautiful estate held by his family north of the spot where the Episcopal Church now stands in Brookline. As proximity to the city was considered desirable, negotiations were also attempted by Mr. Bond and myself, for land on either side of the Western Avenue, on the branch leading to the Punch Bowl. These negotiations, as well as others, failed, either from the high price at which the land was held, or from the reluctance of the owners to acquiesce in the use proposed to be made of the premises.

A tract situated in Cambridge and Watertown, then known as "Stone's Woods," and more familiarly to the college students as "Sweet Auburn," had been sold about this time, and purchased by Mr. George W. Brimmer, — a gentleman whose just appreciation of the beautiful in nature had prompted him to preserve from destruction the trees and other natural features of that attractive spot. He afterwards enlarged the original purchase by adding to it several pieces of front land, intervening between the wood and the public road, on which the gate now stands.

Having often visited Sweet Auburn, both in company with Mr. Brimmer, and anteriorly to his purchase, I now proposed to him, in 1830, the purchase of the whole lot for an ornamental cemetery, like that in contemplation, provided a sufficient number of subscribers could be obtained to cover the expense.   Mr. Brimmer acceded to this proposal, and, although the land had risen in value, and could probably have been sold to private purchasers, at no distant period, for a large advance, he liberally gave me the refusal, for an object of public benefit, at the original cost to himself.   He afterwards became one of the most active members of the first Committee, or Board of Managers.

In the preceding year, 1829, the Massachusetts Horticultural Society had been incorporated by the Legislature.   Among the first officers chosen were Gen. H. A. S. Dearborn, President; Zebedee Cook, Vice-President; and Jacob Bigelow, Corresponding Secretary.   At that time there was no ornamented rural cemetery, deserving of notice, in the United States, and none even in Europe, of a plan and magnitude corresponding to those which Mount Auburn possesses at the present time. Moreover, the subject was new, the public were lukewarm, and, in many cases, the prejudices and apprehensions of the community were strongly opposed to the removal of the dead from the immediate precincts of populous cities and villages to the solitude of a distant wood. There seemed little doubt that, if these prejudices were to be overcome, it would be best done by enlisting in favor of a change, the co-operation of a young, active, and popular society. Under this conviction I brought before the officers of the Horticultural Society the assent of Mr. Brimmer to sell, for a public cemetery, under suitable conditions, the estate which has since become Mount Auburn.* The proposition was favorably received ; and, as the society was at that time destitute of funds adequate to the purchase, measures were taken to see if a subscription could be obtained, from private individuals, sufficient to cover the price of the land. And, in pursuance of this object, meetings were held of persons favorably disposed to the establishment of a cemetery, under the auspices of the Horticultural Society.

The first meeting on this basis was called at the Exchange Coffee House, Nov. 23, 1830, on an

---

* See the Histories of Mount Auburn, by Thacher & Walter; also Gen. Dearborn's Account, published with Dr. Harris' Address before the Horticultural Society, in 1832 ; also the Boston Daily Advertiser, Sept. 9th, 1851, and Boston Atlas, Sept 16th, 1851.

informal notification signed by Jacob Bigelow and
John C. Gray. At this meeting the offer of Mr.
Brimmer to sell Sweet Auburn was announced,
and a committee was appointed, consisting of Gen.
Dearborn, Dr. Bigelow, Edward Everett, George
Bond, J. C. Gray, Abbott Lawrence, and G. W.
Brimmer, to take measures for bringing the subject before the public, and insuring a future and
larger meeting. To accommodate the wishes of
the horticulturists, an experimental garden for
the cultivation of flowers, fruits, &c., was ordered
to form a part in the proposed allotment of the
ground about to be purchased. This garden, however, from the want of specific funds for its support, and from various other causes, never went
into operation.*

During the following winter and spring nothing
was done in promotion of the design, except that,

---

* In Gen. Dearborn's Account, alluded to in the preceding
note, he says : — " Soon after the organization of the Horticultural Society he (Dr. Bigelow) suggested to the President the
expediency of combining a cemetery with an experimental garden." This statement, in part only, is correct. The Cemetery
was suggested by Dr. Bigelow, but the experimental garden
was a suggestion of other officers and members of the Horticultural Society.

as the season opened, many individuals were induced to visit Sweet Auburn, and to become acquainted with the scenery and natural advantages of the spot. Articles explanatory and promotive of the design also appeared in various newspapers. On the eighth of June, 1831, the committee who had the subject in charge called a larger meeting of gentlemen, favorably disposed to the enterprise, at the Horticultural Society's room, in Joy's Building. At this meeting, which was well attended, Judge Story was called to the Chair, and Edward Everett officiated as Secretary. Much interest in the design was expressed by various speakers, and it was voted expedient to purchase the estate offered by Mr. Brimmer, — containing about seventy-two acres, — at six thousand dollars, in behalf of the Horticultural Society, as soon as one hundred subscribers for cemetery lots, at sixty dollars each, should be obtained. A committee of twenty was appointed, with instructions, to report early on a general plan of proceeding, of which committee the following gentlemen were chosen members: — Messrs. Joseph Story, Daniel Webster, H. A. S. Dearborn, Charles Lowell, Samuel Appleton, Jacob Bigelow, Edward Everett, George W. Brimmer, George Bond, A.

H. Everett, Abbott Lawrence, James T. Austin,
Franklin Dexter, Joseph P. Bradlee, Charles
Tappan, Charles P. Curtis, Zebedee Cook, John
Pierpont, L. M. Sargent, and George W. Pratt.
By this committee subscription papers were put in
circulation, and, in a short time, it was found that
three quarters of the requisite amount had been
obtained. The remainder was afterwards procured, chiefly by the exertions of Mr. Joseph P.
Bradlee, one of the Committee. The report of
the Committee to the society, which was accepted,
was as follows : —

" The Committee of the Horticultural Society,
to whom was referred the method of raising subscriptions for the Experimental Garden and Cemetery, beg leave to Report : —

1. That it is expedient to purchase for a
Garden and Cemetery, a tract of land, com-
monly known by the name of Sweet Auburn,
near the road leading from Cambridge to Watertown, containing about seventy-two acres, for
the sum of six thousand dollars ; provided this
sum can be raised in the manner proposed in the
second article of this Report.

2. That a subscription be opened for lots of

ground in the said tract, containing not less than two hundred square feet each, at the price of sixty dollars for each lot, — the subscription not to be binding until one hundred lots are subscribed for.

3. That when a hundred or more lots are taken, the right of choice shall be disposed of at an auction, of which seasonable notice shall be given to the subscribers.

4. That those subscribers, who do not offer a premium for the right of choosing, shall have their lots assigned to them by lot.

5. That the fee of the land shall be vested in the Massachusetts Horticultural Society, but that the use of the lots, agreeably to an act of the Legislature, respecting the same, shall be secured to the subscribers, their heirs, and assigns, forever.

6. That the land devoted to the purpose of a Cemetery shall not contain less than forty acres.

7. That every subscriber, upon paying for his lot, shall become a member for life, of the Massachusetts Horticultural Society, without being subject to assessments.

8. That a Garden and Cemetery Committee,

of nine persons, shall be chosen annually, first by the subscribers, and afterwards by the Horticultural Society, whose duty it shall be to cause the necessary surveys and allotments to be made, to assign a suitable tract of land for the Garden of the Society, and to direct all matters appertaining to the regulation of the Garden and Cemetery; and five at least of this Committee shall be persons having rights in the Cemetery.

9. That the establishment, including the Garden and Cemetery, be called by a definite name, to be supplied by the Committee."

At a meeting of subscribers, called August 3d, 1831, it appeared that one hundred lots in the Cemetery, had, at that time, been taken by subscription; and that, therefore, agreeably to the terms, the subscription had become obligatory. The following gentlemen were then chosen to constitute a board of managers under the name of the Garden and Cemetery Committee: — Messrs. Joseph Story, Henry A. S. Dearborn, Jacob Bigelow, Edward Everett, George W. Brimmer, George Bond, Charles Wells, Benjamin A. Gould, and George W. Pratt. At the same time it was resolved that a public religious consecration should be held upon the grounds, and the following gentlemen were appointed a Committee to make arrangements for that purpose : — Messrs. Joseph Story, Henry A. S. Dearborn, Charles P. Curtis, Charles Lowell, Zebedee Cook, Jr., Joseph T. Buckingham, George W. Brimmer, George W. Pratt, and Z. B. Adams.

At a meeting of the Garden and Cemetery Committee, August 8th, it was voted that General Dearborn, Dr. Bigelow, and Mr. Brimmer, be a Sub-Committee to procure an accurate topographical survey of Mount Auburn, and to report a plan for laying it out into lots. This Sub-Committee engaged the services of Mr. Alexander Wadworth, Civil Engineer, with whose assistance they completed the duty assigned to them.

The public religious consecration of the Cemetery took place on Saturday, September 24th, 1831. A temporary amphitheatre was fitted up with seats, in one of the deep valleys of the wood, having a platform for the speakers erected at the bottom. An audience of nearly two thousand persons were seated among the trees, adding a scene of picturesque beauty to the impressive solemnity of the occasion. The order of performances was as follows : —

1. INSTRUMENTAL MUSIC, by the Boston Band.
2   INTRODUCTORY PRAYER, by Rev. Dr. WARE.
    HYMN,*
    WRITTEN BY THE REV. MR. PIERPONT.
    ,   4. ADDRESS,
    BY THE HON. JOSEPH STORY.†
5. CONCLUDING PRAYER, by the REV. MR. PIERPONT.
    6. MUSIC BY THE BAND.

The following account of the scene is taken
from the Boston Courier of the time : —

"An unclouded sun and an atmosphere purified
by the showers of the preceding night, combined
to make the day one of the most delightful we
ever experience at this season of the year. It is
unnecessary for us to say that the address by
Judge Story was pertinent to the occasion, for if
the name of the orator were not sufficient, the
perfect silence of the multitude, enabling him to
be heard with distinctness at the most distant
part of the beautiful amphitheatre in which the
services were performed, will be sufficient testimony as to its worth and beauty. Neither is it
in our power to furnish any adequate description
of the effect produced by the music of the thou-

---

* See Part II.   † See Part II.

sand voices which joined in the hymn, as it swelled in chastened melody from the bottom of the glen, and, like the spirit of devotion, found an echo in every heart, and pervaded the whole scene.

The natural features of Mount Auburn are incomparable for the purpose to which it is now sacred. There is not in all the untrodden valleys of the West, a more secluded, more natural or appropriate spot for the religious exercises of the living; we may be allowed to add our doubts whether the most opulent neighborhood of Europe furnishes a spot so singularly appropriate for a ' Garden of Graves.'

In the course of a few years, when the hand of Taste shall have passed over the luxuriance of Nature, we may challenge the rivalry of the world to produce another such abiding place for the spirit of beauty. Mount Auburn has been but little known to the citizens of Boston ; but it has now become holy ground, and

Sweet Auburn, loveliest village of the plain,

— a village of the quick and the silent, where Nature throws an air of cheerfulness over the labors of Death, — will soon be a place of more general resort, both for ourselves and for strangers, than any other spot in the vicinity. Where else shall we go with the musings of Sadness, or for the indulgence of Grief; where to cool the burning brow of Ambition, or relieve the swelling heart of Disappointment? We can find no better spot, for the rambles of curiosity, health or pleasure; none sweeter, for the whispers of affection among the living; none lovelier, for the last rest of our kindred."

The following is the contemporaneous description published by order of the Committee, in the appendix to Judge Story's address : —

" The tract of land which received the name of Mount Auburn, is situated on the southerly side of the main road leading from Cambridge to Watertown, and is partly within the limits of each of those towns. Its distance from Boston is about four miles. The place was formerly known by the name of Stone's Woods, the title to most of the land having remained in the family of Stone, from an early period after the settlement of the country. Within a few years, previous to the date of the consecration, the hill and part of the woodland had been offered for sale, and were purchased by

George W. Brimmer, Esq., whose object was to
prevent the destruction of the trees, and to preserve
so beautiful a spot for some public or appropriate
use. The purchase which has now been made
by the Horticultural Society, includes between
seventy and eighty acres, extending from the
road, nearly to the banks of Charles River. A
portion of the land situated next to the road, and
now under cultivation, is intended to constitute
the Experimental Garden of the Horticultural
Society. A long water-course extending between
this tract and the interior woodland, forms a
natural boundary, separating the two sections.
The inner portion, which is set apart for the
purposes of a Cemetery, is covered throughout
most of its extent with a vigorous growth of
forest trees, many of them of large size, and
comprising an unusual variety of kinds. This
tract is beautifully undulating in its surface, containing a number of bold eminences, steep ac-
clivities, and deep shadowy valleys. A remarkable
natural ridge with a level surface runs through
the ground from the south-east to north-west, and
has for many years been known as a secluded and
favorite walk. The principal eminence, called
Mount Auburn in the plan, is one hundred and

twenty-five feet above the level of Charles River,
and commands from its summit one of the finest
prospects which can be obtained in the environs
of Boston.   On one side is the city in full view,
connected at its extremities with Charlestown and
Roxbury.   The serpentine course of Charles
River, with the cultivated hills and fields rising
beyond it, and having the Blue Hills of Milton
in the distance, occupies another portion of the
landscape.   The village of Cambridge, with the
venerable edifices of Harvard University, are
situated about a mile to the eastward.   On the
north, at a very small distance, Fresh Pond appears, a handsome sheet of water, finely diversified by its woody and irregular shores.   Country
seats and cottages seen in various directions, and
especially those on the elevated land at Watertown, add much to the picturesque effect of the
scene.   It is proposed to erect on the summit of
Mount Auburn, a Tower, after some classic model,
of sufficient height to rise above the tops of the
surrounding trees.   This will serve the double
purpose of a landmark to identify the spot from a
distance, and of an observatory commanding an
uninterrupted view of the country around it.
From the foot of this monument will be seen in

detail the features of the landscape, as they are
successively presented through the different vistas
which have been opened among the trees ; while
from its summit, a magnificent and unbroken
panorama, embracing one of the most delightful
tracts in New England, will be spread out beneath the eye. Not only the contiguous country,
but the harbor and bay of Boston, with their
ships and islands, and, in a clear atmosphere,
the distant mountains of Wachusett, and probably even of Monadnock, will be comprehended
within the range of vision.

The grounds of the Cemetery have been laid
out with intersecting avenues, so as to render
every part of the woods accessible. These avenues are curved and variously winding in their
course, so as to be adapted to the natural in-
equalities of the surface. By this arrangement,
the greatest economy of the land is produced,
combining at the same time the picturesque effect
of landscape gardening. Over the more level
portions, the avenues are about twenty feet wide,
and are suitable for carriage roads. The more
broken and precipitous parts are approached
by foot-paths, about six feet in width.   These
passage-ways are to be smoothly gravelled and

planted on both sides with flowers and ornamental
shrubs. Lots of ground, containing each three
hundred square feet, are set off, as family burial
places, at suitable distances on the sides of the
avenues and paths. The perpetual right of inclosing and of using these lots as places of sepulture,
is conveyed to the purchasers of them, by the
Horticultural Society. It is confidently expected
that many of the proprietors will, without delay,
proceed to erect upon their lots such monuments
and appropriate structures as will give to the
place a part of the solemnity and beauty which
it is destined ultimately to acquire.

It has been voted to procure, or construct, a
receiving tomb in Boston, and another at Mount
Auburn, at which, if desired, funerals may ter-
minate, and in which the remains of the deceased
may be deposited, until such time as the friends
shall choose to direct their removal to the Cemetery ; this period, however, not to exceed six
months.

The principal entrance to Mount Auburn will
be through a lofty Egyptian gateway, which it is
proposed to erect on the main road, at the commencement of the Central Avenue. Another
entrance or gateway is provided on the cross-

road at the eastern foot of the hill. Whenever the funds of the corporation shall justify the expense, it is proposed that a small Grecian or Gothic Temple shall be erected on a conspicuous eastern eminence, which in reference to this allotment has received the prospective name of Temple Hill.*

As the designation and conveyance of the lots requires that they should be described with reference to places bearing fixed appellations, it has been found necessary to give names to the avenues, foot-paths, hills, &c. The names which have been adopted, were suggested chiefly by natural objects and obvious associations. Taken in connection with the printed plan, they will be found sufficient to identify any part of the ground, without the probability of mistake."

The avenues and paths of Mount Auburn were laid out by a Sub-Committee, consisting of Messrs. Dearborn, Bigelow, and Brimmer. They were made, as far as possible, to conform to the natural face of the ground. Curved or winding courses were generally adopted, both for picturesque effect, and for easy approach to the various lots. The avenues for carriages were made

* Now occupied by lots. The Chapel is placed elsewhere.

about eighteen feet wide, but the footpaths about five feet; the lots being set back six feet from the path or avenue. The standard or minimum size of a lot, necessary to constitute the owner a proprietor in the Corporation, was fixed by the Trustees at not less than three hundred square feet, or twenty feet by fifteen, which size has never been changed.

The labor of clearing the avenues, &c., and grading the ground, occupied most of the season. Gen. Dearborn zealously devoted himself nearly the whole of this time to the examination of the ground, the laying out of roads, and superintending the workmen. He also transplanted from his own nurseries a large collection of healthy, young forest trees, which he distributed through the entire front of the Cemetery. A part of these have since been moved and re-arranged, constituting one of the most beautiful ornaments of the place. On this occasion, the Garden and Cemetery Committee, on motion of Mr. Brimmer, Dec. 2d, 1831, —

Voted, — " That, in consideration of the very acceptable services rendered by Gen. Dearborn, at Mount Auburn, and for the assiduity he has manifested in carrying into effect the purposes and

designs of the Committee, that the lot selected by
him in the grounds appropriated to the Cemetery,
be presented to him, in behalf of the proprietors,
and that the same shall be conveyed to him and
his heirs in the manner prescribed by the Rules
and Regulations of the Association, as a gratuity,
and that Mr. Cook be requested to notify him of
the same."

At a meeting of the Garden and Cemetery
Committee, Nov. 3d, 1831, it was voted that Dr.
Bigelow be authorized to have a plan of the ground
lithographed, and to give names to such ponds,
avenues, or places as require them; also to alter
any names now affixed. In the execution of this
commission, similar to one previously ordered by
the sub-committee, the names of trees, shrubs, and
plants were mostly adopted, to distinguish the
paths and avenues, and this method has since
been followed, with occasional deviations, made to
gratify the desire of parties interested. A plan of
Mount Auburn, by Mr. Alexander Wadsworth,
was at this meeting submitted and accepted, and
afterwards lithographed on a reduced scale.

At the same meeting it was voted to permit
single interments to be made in the ground by
persons not proprietors. The inclosure, since called

ST. JAMES' lot, on Cypress Avenue, was shortly after set off for the purpose, and inclosed with a slight fence. At a more recent period, after this repository had become full, another inclosure, called ST. JOHN's lot, was laid out on Fir Avenue, in 1848. The original charge for single interments was ten dollars, which was afterwards increased to twelve, with an additional charge of fifty cents for a stone bearing a number corresponding with the name of the occupant recorded in a book kept for the purpose. Adopted Sept. 1st, 1856.

About one hundred lots having been surveyed, it was voted, in 1831, to offer at auction to proprietors, for a premium, the right of choice among the lots laid out. Liberal bids were made at this auction, and a considerable sum was the result. The largest bid was $100, by Mr. Samuel Appleton, and the next, $50, by Mr. Benjamin Adams. The whole proceeds of the sale, after deducting auction expenses, as it appears from the Treasurer's books, were $944.92.

The original price of lots was sixty dollars for three hundred square feet, being twenty cents per foot; and a certain number of lots were kept surveyed, in anticipation of sales, at this price. But it was voted, Nov. 3d, 1831, that, "if an applicant

choose to have a new lot assigned to him, the
Committee may, if they see fit, assign to him a
new lot, on his paying ten dollars additional to his
former dues." The addition was afterwards increased to $20. The price of a surveyed lot was
increased, in 1834, to $65; in 1836, to $80; in
1844, to $100; and in 1854, to $150, — at which
it now remains, with the exception that for certain
choice lots a higher price is required. This progressive increase of price has been founded on the
increased value of the Cemetery, and the differ-
ence in interest to early purchasers.

March 6, 1832. A subscription having been
raised, by ladies in Boston, for the purpose of
erecting a monument to Miss Hannah Adams, it
was voted that the Committee on Surveys appropriate a portion of land for the purpose of deposit-
ing her remains; and, Sept. 2d, the Treasurer was
ordered to pay $35 for an iron fence around her
monument. 'This was the first monument erected
in Mount Auburn Cemetery. The first interment
was that of a child of Mr. James Boyd, on Mountain Avenue, July 6th, 1832. The second was
that of Mrs. Mary Hastings, July 12th, of the
same year.

May —, 1832. Messrs. Cook & Bond were a

Committee to decide upon the form of a temporary
fence to enclose the whole ground at Mount Auburn. A contract was soon afterwards made with
Mr. Leonard Stone to erect a wooden fence, of
rough sawed pales, for which it appears the
whole amount paid him was $2,636.65. This
fence was standing till 1844, when it began to
be superseded by the present iron fence.

THE GATEWAY.

The funds of the Corporation being thought
adequate to the erection of a wooden gateway,
with some reference to ornament, at a meeting of
the Garden and Cemetery Committee, Sept 1st,
1832, it was voted, — "That the model for a gateway and lodges, produced by Dr. Bigelow, be
adopted, and that Gen. Dearborn, Dr. Bigelow,
and Mr. Brimmer, be a Committee to cause the
gate and lodges to be constructed of wood agreeably to said model." This model was intended as
a pattern for a corresponding structure, to be afterwards executed in stone, when the Corporation
should be able to meet the expense. A contract
was made with Mr. M. P. Brazee, of Cambridge-
port, to build a gate on this plan for $1,366. This

wooden gate, painted in imitation of granite, stood
until 1842, when, at a meeting of the Trustees,
Sept. 27th, and in pursuance of the Report of a
Committee of the Trustees, it was voted, — "That
the Committee on Lots — Messrs. Bigelow, Curtis,
and Parker — be empowered to contract with
Octavius T. Rogers, of Quincy, for the building
of a granite gateway at Mount Auburn, and to
pay for the same nine thousand five hundred dollars." The Report alluded to provided for the
reproduction, in stone, of a gate and lodges having
" substantially the same form, model, and dimensions as the present (wooden) gate and lodges."
The Committee, after application to various granite
contractors in Quincy, had found no one, except
Mr. Rogers, who would undertake to make and
raise the cap, or cornice stone, in a single piece.
Mr. Rogers completed his contract in a prompt
and satisfactory manner, the stone cap being raised
to its place with screws on wooden frames. To
prevent accident to the corners a thick bed of
mortar was laid on the stone next below it, which
left, when finished, a large and unseemly joint
between the two principal stones. The Trustees
voted, Sept. 16th, not to accept the gate with this
blemish ; and the mortar was removed by the con-

tractor, with some difficulty, by sawing it out. The gate was then accepted.

The gate is in the Egyptian style, its height being twenty-five feet, and the whole length, including the lodge, sixty feet. The piers or posts are four feet square, the entrance ten feet wide, and the greatest length of the cornice twenty-four feet. Two obelisks are connected with the two lodges by a curved, iron fence. The outline of the gate is mostly taken from some of the best examples in Denderah and Karnac, in which the piers are vertical, and the curve of the cornice vertical in its lower half. The banded cylinder, the foliage of the cornice, and the winged globe, are Egyptian. On the latter a lotus flower is turned over, so as to conceal the head of the fabulous animal with which the ancient examples are usually defaced. The size of the stones, and the solidity of the structure, entitle it to a stability of a thousand years.

On the outside of the gate is this inscription:

THEN SHALL THE DUST RETURN
TO THE EARTH AS IT WAS,
AND THE SPIRIT SHALL RETURN
UNTO GOD WHO GAVE IT.

On the opposite side:

MOUNT AUBURN CONSECRATED
SEPTEMBER 24TH, 1831.

In a year after the consecration of Mount Auburn Cemetery, the success of the enterprise being
considered no longer doubtful, it was deemed desirable to secure the addition of about twenty-four
acres of land, lying on the westerly side of the
first purchase, and belonging to David Stone and
others, and to Ann Cutter. With this view, it was
voted, Sept. 24th, 1832, that "it is expedient to
borrow five thousand dollars to be reimbursed,
with interest, out of the first proceeds of cemetery
lots, and to be applied to the purchase of land
lying on the west side of the Garden and Cemetery, and to the making of improvements in the
Mount Auburn estate." This is believed to be the
only instance, in the history of Mount Auburn, of
a loan being authorized on the part of the Society
or Corporation. The proposed land was purchased
on credit, with notes, secured by mortgage, of the
land acquired, and no lots were sold within it until
this incumbrance was removed. The Corporation
thus obtained about twenty-four acres of valuable
land, the subsequent sale of which has been an important element in its prosperity. The balance of
account soon appeared on the other side, and on
April 14th, 1836, we find a vote, "that the Treasurer be instructed to invest from five to seven

thousand dollars of the funds of this Corporation in some safe and profitable security." Since that time the Treasury has never been without a large surplus at the end of the year, sometimes amounting to $40,000, and upwards.

The accompanying plan, by Mr. Alexander Wadsworth, represents the Mount Auburn land as it existed previously to 1832. Most of the lots laid down had been purchased by Mr. Brimmer, at different times, and were, by him, conveyed to the Horticultural Society, in a general deed, dated Jan. 10th, 1832. But the following additional lots were subsequently purchased by the Society or Corporation from other parties: The lot, marked Cutter, about nine acres, was conveyed by Ann Cutter, Oct. 6th, 1832. The lot, marked D. Stone, about seventeen acres, by David Stone and David Stone, guardian, Jan. 13, 1833. The lot, marked Gould, two acres and a quarter, was purchased at auction by Mr. Gould, one of the Trustees, and by him immediately conveyed to the Corporation, Dec. 20, 1844. The "Stone Farm," about sixteen acres, was not added till 1854, when it was conveyed to the Corporation, by Mr. J. B. Dana, as hereafter shown.

By the surveys and estimates of Mr. Wads-

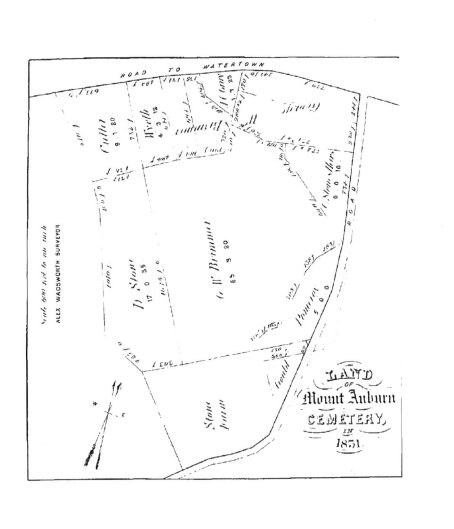

LAND
OF
Mount Auburn
CEMETERY,
IN
1831.

worth, it appears that the whole land now owned
and used as a Cemetery by the Corporation of
Mount Auburn, is a little short of one hundred
and thirty acres.   Certain parcels situated east of
the road, which is now called Coolidge Avenue,
appear to have been conveyed by the Corporation,
at different times, to Winchester, Brazce, and
other parties.   One piece of low land was conveyed to Josiah Coolidge, in consideration of a
ditch to be made by him, with the perpetual right
of drainage through his land to Charles River.

The subject of admission to the Cemetery has,
at different times, been a source of perplexity to
the Trustees.   At first, promiscuous admittance
was allowed to persons on foot, on horseback, and
in carriages.   But, in a short time, great inconvenience was felt from the number of persons, in
pursuit of pleasure, who rode or drove recklessly
through the grounds, to the detriment of the paths
and the annoyance of other visitors.   At a meeting, April 10th, 1832, it was voted that "no horses
or carriages, except those attending on funerals,
will be admitted into the grounds of Mount Auburn."   On the 29th of the same month this
measure was modified by a vote " that the proprietors of lots in the Cemetery be admitted into

the grounds with their vehicles, and that tickets
entitling them and their families to admission be
sent to them, which tickets shall not be transferable, and shall be available for the present year."
Regulations were also prescribed to prevent fast
driving, and to insure the proper fastening of
horses, &c. These Regulations have mainly continued in force to the present time, except that
discretionary power has sometimes been given to
the Gate-keeper to admit strangers; but the abuse
of this privilege, and the influx of improper persons, have caused the Rule to be rescinded, and
tickets are now required of all persons, except
foot passengers.

February 1, 1834. It was voted that Mr.
Bond and Mr. Curtis be a Committee to prepare
a Catalogue of lots and proprietors' names for
publication. This was the first regular Catalogue
published. Catalogues were afterwards printed in
1835, 1838, 1841, 1846, and 1857.

As early as 1834, it became apparent that the
interests of the Horticultural Society and those of
the proprietors of Cemetery lots were not identical.
The question of division of the proceeds of sales
between two objects, — that of defraying the expenses of the Society on the one hand, and that

of the improvement of Mount Auburn on the
other, — was not always easy of adjustment. On
the question of legal and moral right, it was found
that the Horticultural Society held the fee of the
land, and that to them was due whatever credit
belonged to the inception of the undertaking. On
the other hand, it appeared that the number of lot
holders was rapidly increasing; that from them
had been derived most of the funds of the establishment; and that, from their condition of membership, they would soon have a controlling vote
in the affairs of the Society. Considerable warmth
of feeling was elicited among the advocates of the
two parties; and it became evident that a peaceful
arrangement was not likely to be made, except by
a sale of Mount Auburn, by the Horticultural
Society, to a new Corporation, to be composed of
the holders of lots.

For this purpose a Committee was appointed,
consisting of Judge Story, Messrs. Charles P.
Curtis, Elijah Vose, and Marshall P. Wilder.
This Committee held several somewhat excited
sessions without arriving at any agreement, and
were near breaking up their conference without
any practical result, when a compromise appears
to have been effected by the conciliatory efforts of

Mr. Wilder, one of the Committee, and the parties came to an agreement of the following basis, mainly: that the proceeds of all sales of lots shall be divided annually between the Horticultural Society and the new Corporation in such manner that, after deducting fourteen hundred dollars for the expenses of the Cemetery, then one fourth part of the gross proceeds should be paid to the Horticultural Society, and the remaining three fourths should be retained by the Mount Auburn Corporation for its own use. The result of this amicable arrangement, afterwards duly accepted and ratified, has been highly auspicious to both parties concerned. The Horticultural Society has become opulent and prosperous, as it is useful to the public; while the proprietors of Mount Auburn have been able to expend nearly three hundred thousand dollars in the preservation, improvement, embellishment, and enlargement of their Cemetery.

Immediate application was made to the Legislature for an act incorporating the proprietors of the Cemetery, and a deed of conveyance, in which were recited the conditions of the act, was afterwards made out from the Horticultural Society to the newly incorporated proprietors.

It is somewhat remarkable that, at the date of

these important transactions, a gap of more than three months appears in the records of the time. Neither the record books of the Horticultural Society, of the Garden and Cemetery Committee, nor of the Proprietors of Mount Auburn, contain the names of the Committee, nor their report to the Society. The record book of the Horticultural Society has the following statement: — " A report was made on the 23d of January, 1835, by Judge Story, to the Horticultural Society, and accepted, as appears by the record of that day, comprising the agreement finally made between these parties. This report cannot be found. In its absence, therefore, the views of the parties must be sought principally in an act of the Legislature, of March 31, 1835, and a vote of the Society, June 6, 1835, and also in the deed to the Mount Auburn Proprietors." At the top of the same page it is stated that, " The following portions of records are mostly taken from the New England Farmer, and are entered here in pursuance of a vote passed by the Society."

The act of incorporation having been assented to by the proprietors, under their individual signatures, a meeting was called by the persons named in the act on the 21st of April, 1835, at which the

Hon. John Davis was chosen Moderator, and
Charles P. Curtis, Esq., Secretary. Judge Story
was appointed a Committee to prepare such By-
Laws as he should deem necessary. It was voted
to proceed to the choice, by ballot, of nine Trustees, and the following gentlemen were declared
to be elected, viz. : Joseph Story, Samuel Appleton, George Bond, Jacob Bigelow, Benjamin A.
Gould, Charles Brown, Charles P. Curtis, James
Read, and Joseph P. Bradlee. It was then voted
that the Trustees be authorized to procure and
accept a conveyance from the Massachusetts
Horticultural Society, of all the lands, tenements,
and personal estate held by them in Cambridge,
Watertown, or elsewhere, appertaining to the
Garden and Cemetery of Mount Auburn.

At an adjourned meeting, April 23d, 1835, the
Hon. Joseph Story was chosen President; George
Bond, Esq., Treasurer; and Benjamin R. Curtis,
Esq., Secretary. The salary of the Secretary
was fixed at one hundred dollars. Messrs. Bond,
Bigelow, and C. P. Curtis were appointed a
Committee on laying out and discontinuing lots.
Messrs. Story and Curtis were appointed a Com-
mittee on Regulations concerning visitors, &c.
Messrs. Bigelow and Story a Committee to devise
a seal for the Corporation.

In September, 1838, Mr. George W. Brimmer died at Florence, in Italy. The following obituary notice appeared in the Boston Daily Advertiser of the time : —

" Although for several years past the subject of this notice has been absent, with the exception of short intervals, from his home, yet the image of his presence, and the sound of his familiar voice, seem to us as but of yesterday. A vivid remembrance of our past gratification accompanies and enhances the sadness attendant on its loss.

Mr. Brimmer, after the termination of his academical studies, in 1803, directed his attention to mercantile pursuits, to which occupation he continued attached for several years. But a natural and highly cultivated taste for the fine arts laid strong claims on his attention and time, and to these elegant pursuits he devoted a large portion of that leisure which his fortune and position enabled him to command. In painting he was both a personal proficient and an accomplished connoisseur, distinguished by the chasteness and almost the severity of his discriminating taste. To architecture he directed a large share of his attention, and has left practical results to attest the beauty of his conceptions. Trinity Church and the facade to the Tremont Theatre,* in Boston, the Unitarian Church in Plymouth, with some other classical structures, are monuments of his genius and the nice discernment which he possessed of fitness in art.

The public spirit of Mr. Brimmer has, on various occasions, been conspicuously manifested in provisions for the general good. When the tract of land, now known as Mount Auburn, was, many years since, offered at auction sale, it was purchased by Mr. Brimmer, and held by him for some years, not for his private use or gratification, but merely to preserve that beautiful woodland from destruction until some appropriate use should be found for it. When the plan of an ornamental cemetery was first suggested, he liberally conveyed the estate for that purpose, at some personal sacrifice, and co-operated with activity in perfecting a place which is now the acknowledged pride of our metropolis.

To the Boston Athenæum Mr. Brimmer has been, for many years, an efficient and active friend. The splendid collection of works on the fine arts, possessed by that institution, was, in a

---

* Afterwards burnt and differently rebuilt.

great measure, formed under his advice and assistance. A few months before his death he sent out from Europe, as a donation to that library, a large number of costly and elegant works, selected by himself during his travels on the Continent, and previously wanting on the shelves of the institution.

In the society in which he moved, Mr. Brimmer will long be recollected for the friendly spirit, and cheerful equanimity, which spoke in his countenance and animated his conversation. An unconstrained and playful vivacity increased the interest of his discourse, which was at all times rational, cultivated and intellectual. An extensive observer of men and manners, he contributed to the entertainment of his friends from the funds of a polished mind, stored by travel and experience. And although free and independent in the expression of his opinions, and uncompromising in his estimate of integrity and truth, yet the courteousness of his manner, and sincerity of his heart, drew around him many friends, who sought and enjoyed his society, as they now cherish his memory."

December 22*d*, 1838. The Trustees voted that it is inexpedient to make gratuitous appropriations of land for the erection of monuments to distinguish individuals. Previously to this vote land had, in several instances, been granted for such purposes.

At the proprietor's meeting, Feb. 4th, 1839, it was voted to increase the number of Trustees to ten, and the name of Samuel T. Armstrong was added to those of the previous Board. This arrangement continued till 1841, when the number of Trustees was again reduced to nine. In 1856 it was increased to twelve, which number still continues.

In 1842, Mr. George Bond died. He had been an active promoter of the enterprise from the earliest stage of its announcement, — even before Sweet Auburn was thought of as its location. He had also served the Corporation as Treasurer, without compensation, for eleven years. On this occasion it was voted by the Trustees, " That the President be requested to communicate to the family of the late George Bond, Esq., the assurance of the sincere sympathy of the Trustees in their recent bereavement, and to express their grateful acknowledgment, on behalf of the proprietors of the Cemetery, of the faithful and valuable services of their friend and associate, as one of the Founders and Trustees of the Cemetery, and as Treasurer of the Corporation since its establishment." Mr. George W. Bond was soon after chosen to succeed his father in the office of Treasurer.

July 15*th*, 1843. The Trustees voted that all sums received from grants or bequests, for the purpose of keeping lots in repair, shall form one fund, to be called the " Fund for Repairs." This vote, after receiving various modifications, in subsequent years, has been gradually matured into what is called the " Repair Fund " in the printed code of By-Laws.

At the same meeting a Committee was ordered to employ an engineer to ascertain the practicability of bringing water from Fresh Pond to Mount Auburn. As the result of this inquiry, it was ascertained, by levels and surveys taken by Mr. Alexander Wadsworth, that the surface of Fresh Pond is several feet lower than the surface of the water in most of the ponds in Mount Auburn.

September 16*th*, 1843. A Committee of five — Messrs. Story, Bigelow, M. Brimmer, Crockett, and Curtis — were ordered to report on " the various improvements which it may be deemed expedient to make upon the grounds of the Cemetery."

This appointment gave rise to an elaborate report from the Committee, through their Chairman, Judge Story, which was presented and accepted at the following meeting, Sept. 29th. It is worthy to be inserted entire, as it marks a period in which it was found that a judicious expenditure of the surplus current income of the Corporation, in permanent improvement, had the effect to increase the number, and thereby promote the interest, of the proprietors.

REPORT.

" The Committee to whom was referred the report of a Committee on the subject of introducing fresh water into the grounds of Mount Auburn, with directions to take into consideration the various improvements which it may be deemed expedient to make there, have had the same under their consideration, and respectfully report. That by the act of incorporation of the Proprietors of the Cemetery of Mount Auburn, the moneys which shall arise from the sale of the lots, and belong to the Corporation, are required to be forever devoted and applied to the preservation, improvement, embellishment, and enlargement of the said Cemetry and the incidental expenses thereof: — that hitherto these purposes have been faithfully adhered to, the grounds have been laid out, and paths and avenues have been established, a house with suitable appendages built, a temporary gateway erected, and a suitable temporary fence inclosing the grounds. During the present year a permanent granite gateway has been substituted for the former wooden one. After deducting all the expenses hitherto incurred, including the expense of the granite gateway, there will remain at the end of the present year in the treasury, according to the statement made to the Committee by the treasurer, the sum of about twenty-six thousand dollars applicable to the general objects contemplated in the act of incorporation.

It is well known, that among these objects there are some which have always from the beginning of the Cemetery been deemed of primary importance, and to which the funds of the Corporation were designed to be applied as soon as any adequate surplus should exist. Indeed these objects were held out to the original subscribers as the main inducements for their patronage and encouragement of the enterprise, and without them little or no success could have been hoped for. The Committee, therefore, deem it their sacred duty to recommend that these objects should be put in a train to secure their entire accomplishment as early as the funds of the Corporation shall enable the Trustees to do so. The Committee beg leave to state that the objects to which they have alluded, are, 1. The erection of a permanent stone or iron fence upon the front grounds of the Cemetery, and a hedge fence on the remaining three sides thereof, for their due protection and security. 2. The draining of the low grounds, and the introduction of pure water which should run into the grounds and through the ponds within the same, into Charles River. 3. The erection of a suitable granite chapel where the religious services for the dead may be suitably performed, and which also in the interior sides may become the repository of marble busts and statues and other sepulchral monuments, which may from time to time be placed there by liberal benefactors and friends in memory of the dead, and which would not bear the exposure of the open air in our climate. 4. The erection of a granite tower or observatory on the summit of Mount Auburn, from which the entire grounds of the Cemetery, and the whole range of the adjacent country may be distinctly seen, — these objects, in the opinion of the Committee, may all be attained within a few years by devoting the present funds of the Corporation to them, and such additional funds as from past experience the Committee are justified in believing, will unquestionably come into the treasury within the same period of years. Which of these objects have a priority, or whether all of them should be simultaneously undertaken and a proportion of the present funds applied *pro rata* to each, is a matter for the ultimate decision of the Trustees; and it is not improbable that for some of these objects, private subscriptions may be obtained from munificent individuals in aid of such funds as the Trustees may devote to the purpose.

The Committee ask leave to suggest some considerations for the deliberation of the Trustees, which have occurred to them, and which may confirm some of the statements already suggested.

1. As to a permanent fence. It is believed by the Committee that a permanent iron fence, with a suitable granite foundation, can be erected of a suitable height, on the whole length of the Cemetery fronting on the Cambridge and Watertown public highway, for an expense not exceed-

ing $17,000. The other three sides of the Ceme-
tery the Committee propose should be inclosed
by a hedge of buckthorn or some other shrub
thickly planted within and near the present
wooden fence.

This would, in a few years, with suitable care,
constitute a substantial and beautiful inclosure, and
might be done at an expense not exceeding $1000.

2. As to draining the grounds and obtaining a supply of pure water, the various ponds
may be made to communicate with each other,
and the stagnant water be drawn off from
the same by suitable ditches, so as ultimately to
pass through the low ground into Charles River.
The ponds can then be excavated, and the material obtained therefrom be applied to fertilize the
ground on the borders of the Cemetery, and good
gravel bottoms be substituted in the ponds, or if
deemed necessary, or expedient, the ponds can be
partially filled up or narrowed in their area. The
Committee estimate the expense of accomplishing
this part of the plan at not exceeding $3000.

In respect to the conveying of pure water into
the grounds, the Committee are aware of some
difficulty. The most probable source of supply
is from Fresh Pond, by means of an apparatus

to raise the water above the level of the pond in the Cemetery, and then to conduct it through the intermediate lands into the Cemetery and thence to Charles River. To accomplish this object some legislative action will probably be necessary, as well as the consent of the proprietors through whose land the water must pass. A survey of the Pond and of those lands has been already made, and an estimate of the probable expense will be found in the report of the former Committee, which has been recommitted to this Committee, and to which reference is to be had for a more full undertaking of the project and other incidental matters.

3. The erection of a chapel. The Committee deem this a very desirable object. The chapel ought, in their opinion, to be built in a chaste style and taste, and of the most durable materials, and upon a plan which will admit of great additions and enlargements at a future period without injury to the symmetry and proportions of the original building, when the religious services and the erection of monuments therein shall require such additions and enlargements. If the chapel should now be erected of a suitable height of ashlar granite, it may be lighted

by a dome, or lantern, or skylight on the top, and the four sides be reserved for busts, and statues, and monuments. The accommodations for the religious services may be by a moveable pulpit and moveable seats to be placed in such positions as the occasion may require. The chapel, when built, may, if it is thought best to constitute the nave or part of the nave of a future church which shall become with its future transepts a Latin or Greek cross. As has been already suggested, private subscriptions may probably be obtained to aid in the accomplishment of this object. Probably the whole expense of such a chapel for the present purposes of a Cemetery would not exceed $5000.

4. The erection of a tower or observatory. It is believed by the Committee that this may be accomplished at a very moderate expense, and yet be built of the most permanent materials; and it will be a great convenience, and an ornament to the grounds. A round tower of ashlar granite may be built fifty feet high, and of a proper diameter suitable for an easy ascent and descent, at an expense not exceeding $7000.

The Committee are also of opinion, that it is unnecessary to reserve out of the present funds of the Corporation a sum exceeding $3000, to meet any incidental expenditures of the Cemetery, before new funds will accrue; and it is but a just compliance with the known intention of the proprietors to appropriate the residue to one or more or all the objects already indicated.

The Committee beg leave to add, that in making the appropriations of the funds of the Corporation for the purposes aforesaid, they have not lost sight of their duty to reserve out of the fund which may arise from the sales of the lots, a sum sufficient to ensure in perpetuity the improvement, preservation, and ornament of the Cemetery, and the payment of the incidental expenses thereof. They are aware that the number of lots which will remain on hand, will be every year diminishing, and therefore that it will be necessary to make suitable provision to meet the time when they can no longer expect to realize any new funds. That time, however, must be distant, and the lots now on hand are more than sufficient to meet all the future expenditures which may be required for any of the purposes to which they have been referred.

All which is respectfully submitted by the Committee.

JOSEPH STORY, *Chairman.*"

The foregoing report being accepted, the Trustees voted to proceed at once to the erection " of an iron fence on the whole front of the Cemetery, of similar construction and character with the portion of fence now erected, (viz., the curved part next the gate) varying in such particulars as the Committee may see fit, provided the same can be done at an expense not exceeding $15,000, and to be completed in three years from the time of the contract."

THE IRON FENCE.

The curved iron fence which forms a part of the design of the gateway extending from the lodges to the obelisks, and also the whole straight fence which encloses the north and east sides, are essentially Egyptian in their character. The constituent parts are selected from among the emblems and trophies, which are sculptured on various structures extant on the banks of the Nile. The pales of the curved fence are ten feet high, and two inches in diameter. Those of the residue of the front fence are somewhat lighter, being about nine feet high, and one inch and seven eighths in diameter. The whole is supported on short posts of granite once in ten feet, the tops of which rise a foot and a half above the ground, while the bases extend four feet under ground, and are three feet in their transverse diameter at bottom. They have thus a strong foothold independent of the earth about them, and would continue to stand if this earth were removed.

The trellis bars which support the pales are mortised into the stone posts and confined by a cement of melted sulphur. During the last year it was found that the ends of the iron bars were much corroded by the action of the acid formed from the sulphur and atmospheric oxygen. To arrest this destructive process, the mortise holes have been filled with Portland cement, by which it is expected to neutralize the excess of acid, and protect the iron and remaining sulphureous cement from further contact with the atmosphere. The fence was painted in 1845 and 1851, and not again till 1859.

The contract for building the front fence, about 2470 feet in length, was made, in 1844, with Messrs. Adams & Whittredge, and Cummings & Co. for the iron work, and O. T. Rogers for the stone posts, for the aggregate sum of $12,400, of which the iron cost $9800, and the stone posts,

4

$2600. A few lengths of return fence on the south side were not included in this contract.

A contract was made, January 5, 1849, with Messrs. Bryant & Blaisdell, to erect a palisade or wooden fence on the eastern, southern, and western sides of the Cemetery, for $1.48 per foot. In consequence of an application from William P. Winchester, Esq., who offered to contribute $500 toward the expense, the wooden fence was stopped on the east side, or Coolidge Avenue, and an iron fence contracted for in its place. The contract was made Oct. 18th, 1849, with Messrs. C. W. Cummings and G. W. Smith, to build this iron fence for $10,300, the length being 1,624 feet.

The wooden palisade was carried round the south and west sides. In the following winter several rods of the pales which had been set in a bog at the south-west corner, fell down. They were afterwards replaced at a considerable expense by resetting them on sleepers sunk and secured in the mud.

1845. This year the country experienced an unusual loss in the death of Judge Story. Among the objects of attention which filled up the measure of his indefatigable life, Mount Auburn had always held a place. He was chairman of the first large meeting called by the Horticultural Society, and was afterwards President of the corporation of proprietors for eleven years. He made frequent visits to the grounds of the Cemetery, and took great delight in witnessing and promoting their improvement. When not absent from the State, he was punctual in his attendance on the meetings of the Trustees, which were often arranged to meet his convenience.

At a meeting of the Trustees, Sept. 12th, 1845, the following resolutions were offered by Dr. Bigelow, and unanimously adopted :—

" The Trustees of Mount Auburn Cemetery, deeply affected by the event which has taken from them their presiding head, and from society one of its most beloved and distinguished ornaments, are anxious that some suitable memorial should be placed in remembrance of his worth, upon a spot which was loved and frequented by him in life, and to the improvement of which he devoted much of his time and ardent interest.

Therefore voted, that the Trustees offer to the friends and fellow citizens of the deceased a place in the new Chapel now in the progress of erection at Mount Auburn, for the erection of a marble statue of Joseph Story, when such a work worthy of the character of the original shall have been completed through the contributions of the public."

It was also voted that a Committee of three be appointed to take order as to the statue of Judge Story. Messrs. Bigelow, M. Brimmer, and C. P. Curtis were appointed to constitute said Committee. A further account will be found under the head of "Statues," page 68.

At a meeting of the Trustees, January 31st, 1848, the following vote was passed: — "Whereas the Trustees of the subscribers to the statue of the late Dr. Bowditch have paid the customary price for the land on which the statue now stands, therefore, voted, that all the land included within the exterior side of the fence around said statue be, and the same is hereby appropriated and dedicated forever to the use and purpose of sustaining and protecting the said statue."

This statue had been erected under difficulties from the proceeds of a subscription raised soon after the death of Dr. Bowditch, in 1838. The Committee having charge of the work had contracted with Mr. Ball Hughes for a bronze statue to be delivered within a certain time. Mr. Hughes completed the model, but failed to produce the bronze casting. The Committee, after waiting a number of years and repeatedly extending the time of the contract, at length broke off their negotiation with Mr. Hughes, and declared the contract void. Mr. Hughes, however, persevered, and with the assistance of a benevolent friend, at length completed an imperfect casting, which the subscribers thought proper to accept. Of its present condition, an opinion may be formed from the following vote of the Trustees, May 10th, 1853: — " Voted, that a Committee of one be appointed to cause the statue of Dr. Bowditch to be repaired by stopping the holes and painting the whole of a bronze color." It is to be hoped that this memorial to the memory of a distinguished philosopher and citizen, of which the design is better than the execution, may be restored, as it can only be, by a new casting to be sought from those who venerate his memory.

The drainage of the wet and sunken parts of the land has from time to time occupied the attention of the Trustees. A tract of wet land called Wyeth's Meadow, situated on the north side of the Watertown road, is now drained by a culvert which passes under the road into the grounds of Mount Auburn. The water, which was formerly above the surface, now flows through a large stone drain along the easterly side of the *lawn*, crossing Central Avenue, and thence coinciding with

Culvert Avenue along the northerly side of Indian Ridge, till it crosses it at a point opposite the bridge which has been built over Auburn Lake. The cut which has here been made through Indian Ridge is intended to constitute a subterranean passage, both sides of which will be occupied with columbaria, or, as they are here called, catacombs, to be built for sale by the Corporation.

Another stone drain, built in 1843, leads from Forest Pond into Auburn Lake. It passes under the bend of Willow Avenue, and discharges its water in a stream or fall for two thirds of the year under a marble shell into the last mentioned lake.

THE CHAPEL.

From the time of the foundation of Mount Auburn, a design was entertained and often expressed, to erect, as soon as the funds of the Corporation should permit it, a chapel or temple which might serve as a place for funeral solemnities when desired, and as a depository for appropriate monumental works of art. In pursuance of this design, after various preliminary discussions, the Trustees at their meeting, October 15th, 1844, voted to proceed to the erection of such an edifice. It was

voted that it be made " of fine hammered Quincy
granite, and that the Building Committee consist of
Jacob Bigelow, Charles P. Curtis, and James
Read, with power to sign the contracts on behalf of
this Corporation, for erecting the chapel at an expense not exceeding twenty-five thousand dollars."
As the funds were not at that time adequate to the
expense of a structure like that contemplated, it
was voted to solicit a subscription from among the
proprietors, with a view to supply the deficient
amount.   Judge Story, Dr. Bigelow, and Martin
Brimmer, Esq., were appointed a Committee for
this purpose.   This Committee made application to
various public spirited individuals, and obtained
from them a contribution amounting to nearly
$7000.   Among these, Samuel Appleton and Dr.
G. C. Shattuck gave $1000 each, and liberal do-
nations were received from various other persons.

In selecting a design for the Chapel, the Trustees applied to a number of the principal architects
of the city, and received from them half a dozen
different plans.   These were affixed to the wall of
a room, having the names of the authors concealed.
Another supernumerary plan by Dr. Bigelow, was
inserted among the rest.   The Trustees, as yet ig-
norant of the names, proceeded to designate their

preference by marking. All the Trustees, except one, gave their marks for the supernumerary plan, and the only dissentient, Mr. M. Brimmer, afterwards changed his vote, making the decision unanimous.

The Building Committee issued their specifications, and received proposals from various granite workers in Boston and Quincy. The lowest proposal was that of Messrs. O. T. Rogers and Richards & Munn, who offered to furnish and put up the stone work of the building, conformably to the specification, for $19,623. The Committee accepted this proposal, relying on the established character of the contractors, and the fact that Mr. Rogers had served them satisfactorily in the erection of the stone gateway. Subsequently, however, the contractors, finding, probably, that they had under-estimated the expense, endeavored to protect themselves from loss, by underletting certain portions of the work to less responsible parties. The consequence was, that many imperfect, defective, and blemished stones were inserted in the work, so that when the walls were erected, and before the roof was made, the Committee refused to pay any further instalments, or to accept the building, if finished in its then existing state. The contractors,

VIEW FROM THE LAWN.

however, thought it best to go on and complete the
Chapel at their own risk. The Trustees refused
to accept the building; but two or three years
afterwards they appointed a Committee, consisting
of Messrs. Read and Crockett, with power to settle
the disputed account. This Committee made an
adjustment by paying the claim of the contractors
subject to the performance of certain repairs, and
the abatement of $1000 from the amount of their
bill.

The departures made by the builders from the
requirements of the specification and plans, consisted not merely in the introduction of stones
which became rusty in a few months, but in the
employment, in many cases, of stones of such short
dimensions, that they did not sufficiently cover or
overlay each other, so as to be capable of excluding
water. The consequence was a frequent leakage
in storms, with a freezing of the water in winter, greatly impairing the stability of the walls.
After many fruitless attempts in different ways to
repair the leaks, the Trustees voted, August 2d,
1853, on the motion of Mr. Gould, "That it is expedient that the Chapel in Mount Auburn be taken
down for the purpose of rebuilding it in a more safe
and substantial manner." A Committee, consisting

of Messrs. Bigelow, Little, and Tisdale, were appointed, with full powers to carry this vote into effect. This Committee contracted with Messrs. Whitcher and Sheldon, of Quincy, to take down and rebuild the entire Chapel with certain additional stones and new decorations, conducing both to its stability and improved appearance, for $16,900. In reconstructing the edifice, about two hundred blemished or defective stones were removed, and replaced with others of proper size and character. Suitable bonds and joints are everywhere introduced, and large granite ties connecting the clerestory with the outer walls are inserted under the roof. Some of the windows and mouldings have been changed, and the row of leaves beneath the cornice is carried round the buttresses. The Chapel is now a strong and safe building, the decorations are increased, while the aggregate expense for its building and reconstruction, is probably not much, if at all, greater than the sum which such an edifice would cost at the present day. Exclusive of the subscription, the actual cost to the proprietors is still less.

The principal windows of the Chapel are of stained glass, manufactured by Messrs. Ballantyne Allan, of Edinburgh.

CHAPEL IN FRONT.

VIEW FROM CONSECRATION DELL.

A well and pump for the refreshment of visitors have stood for many years near the gate. At a meeting July 6th, 1852, "Mr. Tisdale presented drawings and a plan for a pump and pump-house to be constructed near the gate within the grounds of the Corporation, and it was voted that the same be referred to the Committee who have the subject of constructing the tower in charge, with full powers." The Committee proceeded to construct a new well and pump, with a drain, and stone platform, covered by a small wooden octagonal building with seats inside, after the plans offered by Mr. Tisdale and designed by Mr. Theodore Voelckers. The cost of this building was about $3000.

THE TOWER.

"At a meeting of the Trustees, June 1st, 1852, after some remarks, by the President, on the subject of the contemplated improvements at the Cemetery, the erection of a tower coming next in order, according to the original scheme, it was voted that the President, with Messrs. Gould and Little, be a Committee to prepare plans and estimates for a tower at Mount Auburn, and to report hereafter i. .iting."

At the next meeting, July 6th, Dr. Bigelow, in behalf of the Committee, exhibited a model, designed by him, and approved by the Committee; after due examination of which, the Trustees, on motion of Mr. Crockett, voted " That the plan and model, now presented, be adopted by this Board." And, on motion of Mr. Read, it was also voted, " That Messrs. Bigelow, Little, and Tisdale, be a Committee, with full power, to go on and erect the tower now adopted, in granite."

The Committee, above named, contracted with Messrs. Whitcher & Sheldon, of Quincy, to erect the tower, in stone, for $18,500. But the subsequent addition of stone steps, on several sides, and a broad stone platform about the base, together with the grading of the hill, increased the expense to about $22,000.

The tower is sixty-two feet in height above the summit of Mount Auburn. It is built on the general plan of some of the round towers of the feudal ages, and contains a gallery, battlements, Gothic windows, and a spiral staircase of stone. The stones are smooth hammered on both sides, so that each stone makes a part of both the inside and outside surface of the wall. The horizontal surfaces of all the stones being level and true, it is impossible that any structure, of the same materials, should be more substantial. The summit being above the tops of the highest trees, gives, from its platform, a panoramic view of the Cemetery and surrounding country. A landscape of cities and villages, interspersed with woods, cultivated fields, and large sheets of water, constitutes this view. Charles River, with its various windings, is seen for seven or eight miles of its course, from Boston to Watertown, traversing the level marsh, which, in the distance, looks like a shaven lawn. In clear weather, the horizon is marked by the remote summits of Wachusett, and other distant mountains.

The tower of Mount Auburn serves farther as a landmark, by which the place of the Cemetery is designated in the distance. It identifies the spot which is already the resting place of thousands. It is a centre to which mourning hearts and eyes are daily turned, of those who would fain seek in its shadow for what remains on earth of their children and kindred.

THE STATUES.

At the meeting of the Trustees, Jan. 3d, 1854, the subject of occupying the interior of the Chapel with historical statues of public men was introduced by the President, in the following Report : —

"The great and progressive demand for burial lots in Mount Auburn, which, in the last year, has increased beyond any former precedent, has been attended with a correspondent increase in the funds of the Corporation. This increase has not only been sufficient to carry to their completion nearly all the great works proposed in the original design, but has left, at the end of the year, an accumulated surplus in the Treasurer's hands, for which no demand has been made. It seems proper, at this stage of affairs, that the Trustees should consider what is likely to be the amount of their future receipts, and what destination can most fitly be made of the same, so as to carry out the original objects for which Mount Auburn was instituted, and to answer the just expectation of its proprietors.

The following estimate may serve as the ground of an approximative calculation of the value of future sales of land at Mount Auburn : —

The inclosure of the Cemetery contains about one hundred and ten acres, of which less than ten should be deducted for water and other unavailable portions, leaving one hundred acres. Of this, it is computed that about half is already sold, leaving unsold, fifty acres.

An acre contains   .   .   43,560 sq. ft.

Deduct half this for paths and spaces,

    leaving, say,   .   .   .   21,000 " "

Which, at $33\frac{1}{2}$ cents a foot, the pres-

    ent price is $7,000

And 50 acres are eventually worth   . $350,000

From this is to be deducted about twenty per cent. paid to the Horticultural Society, against which may be offset the premium of twenty per cent. now paid by purchasers, who select their lots. It is apparent that the means of the Corporation are likely to be sufficient for any reasonable improvements, which they may feel themselves justified in undertaking.

The object of the present Report is to submit to the Trustees the expediency and propriety of procuring to be made by competent artists a certain number of marble statues, commemorative of men who have been distinguished in the history of the country by their characters and public services, with a view to these statues being placed within the Chapel, which is now about to be reconstructed. By the charter of the Cemetery, the Corporation are authorized to expend their funds among other objects, for the 'improvement and embellishment' of the place. And one of the proposed objects for which the Chapel was erected, as expressed in Judge Story's Report, entered on our records, was, that 'the interior sides may become the repository of busts, statues, and other sepulchral monuments, which may, from time to time, be placed there.' The custom of placing works of sculpture, commemorative of the illustrious dead, in the interior of chapels and churches, is not uncommon in Europe, and is occasionally seen in this country. And, as such memorials are, or should be, elaborate works of art, the propriety becomes apparent, that they should be protected from the elements by the shelter of a roof.

But few of the distinguished men of our own country, and especially of this section of it, have received from their posterity those permanent marks of gratitude, to which the importance of their public services has entitled them. Having died, perhaps, during the comparative poverty of the country, their merits and claims to such recognition have been obscured by the lapse of years, and for a time forgotten. There were among them men of high intellect, indomitable courage, and unquestioned patriotism, — such qualities as civilized nations, in all ages, have been prompt to recognize and commemorate by lasting memorials. Is it right that we, into whose hands Providence has thrown the appropriate means, should withhold from them this late, yet fitting, tribute, in the midst of a prosperity, founded on their efforts and sacrifices, and which now furnishes us the means to prepare and decorate sumptuous resting places, in life and death, for our own less worthy selves.

If the patronage of genius be permitted to weigh as a collateral consideration, we have artists, resident among us, and others have gone out from our midst, who have already won applause from those who are qualified to judge, and have given proofs that the field, and not the talent, is wanting to their honorable success.

It will be remembered that the Cemetery of Mount Auburn was the first to embody, for its own purposes, a plan, uniting the beauties of

art and nature in a manner, and on a scale,
which had not been effected in this country,
nor, in some respects, in any other. Its fortunate
inception, and well considered arrangements, have
caused it to be imitated in almost all the large
cities and villages of the United States. It remains to be seen whether, from its ample means,
it shall continue to take the lead in carrying
into effect new forms of grateful remembrance
of the dead, or wait to become the tardy imitator
of other institutions, to which it has hitherto
been an example.

  (Signed)   Jacob Bigelow."

On receipt of the above Report, the Trustees
voted, " That a Committee of three, of whom the
President shall be Chairman, be appointed to consider the report on statuary made this day, and
report at a future meeting of the Trustees, upon
the general subject of introducing statues into the
Cemetery at the expense of the Corporation." Mr.
Parker requested that his vote, dissenting from the
foregoing vote, should be entered on record. The
President, with Messrs. Read and Curtis, were
ordered to constitute said Committee.

  At the meeting, Feb. 13th, 1854, the President,

from the Committee on Statuary, made a written report, which was postponed for consideration until the next meeting, the Secretary in the meantime to furnish each Trustee with a copy of the same.

After a discussion of the subject, which was continued through several successive meetings, at length, at the meeting holden Sept. 4th, 1854, the Trustees voted, " That the sum of fifteen thousand dollars be appropriated for the purchase of three marble statues, to be procured and executed under contracts to be made with proper artists ; said statues to be those of persons distinguished in American history. But this vote is subject to the following conditions, viz., that it shall be approved in writing by five at least of this Board of Trustees ; and, second, that the professional opinions of C. P. Curtis, Esq., and the Secretary, shall be taken in writing, and found to sustain the legality of such appropriation." Mr. Crockett requested that his name should be recorded as against the passage of this vote.

Finally, at a meeting, Oct. 2d, 1854, it was declared that, " The vote passed at the last meeting on the subject of statuary, had received the approval of certain Trustees in writing, as follows : ' On the above named conditions, the subscribers,

Trustees of Mount Auburn Cemetery, approve the appropriation of fifteen thousand dollars as above specified, for the above named object.' Signed,

JACOB BIGELOW,
JAMES READ,
ISAIAH BANGS,
B. A. GOULD,
CHARLES P. CURTIS,
CHARLES C. LITTLE,
GEORGE H. KUHN,

Seven in all of the nine Trustees.

The foregoing certificate was annexed to a certified copy of the vote."

About this time, and before the pending questions were definitely settled, a statue of the late Judge Story, destined for Mount Auburn, had arrived from Italy, and was temporarily placed in the vestibule of the Boston Athenæum. It was the result of a spontaneous private subscription which had immediately followed the death of that distinguished citizen and jurist, which happened in 1845, as already noticed on page 52.

As soon as the subscription for this statue had been filled, a meeting of the subscribers was called at the Secretary's office, Nov. 25th, 1845, at which a unanimous vote was passed, " That the Trustees of the Cemetery of Mount Auburn be, and hereby are, appointed a Committee to carry out the views of the subscribers in this matter, and, in case of any exigency, to call another meeting of the subscribers as they shall see fit."

Thereupon, the Trustees of Mount Auburn voted, "That the Trustees will accept the commission so entrusted to them by the subscribers to the fund for the erection of a marble statue of the late Joseph Story, and act under the same accordingly."

The money subscribed was collected and placed at interest, and a contract was made by the Trustees with William W. Story, son of the deceased, to execute a marble statue of his father, deliverable in five years. Owing to various casualties, the statue was not completed in the prescribed time. The contract expired and was renewed, and finally the statue arrived in 1855, about ten years from the time of its being ordered.

The selection of three historical personages to fill the remaining niches of the Chapel, was not an easy task. Much difficulty was felt, particularly in selecting from among the great names which cluster about the period of the American revolution. The Committee entrusted with this responsibility consulted by letter many of our best historians and scholars, without obtaining even an approach to a unanimous result. At last a method was adopted of assuming a representative man for each of four great periods, or important epochs, in the history of Massachusetts. The first era was that of the settlement of the colony, and is represented in the person of John Winthrop, its first governor. The second period was that of the first resistance to the aggressions of the British parliament, of which movement James Otis was the leader and impersonation. The third epoch comprised the revolution itself and the establishment of a new constitution, a momentous period, fitly represented in the person of John Adams. Lastly, the fourth, or present period, which is that of peaceful fruition under the supremacy of beneficial laws, finds a just embodiment in the character of the conservative and eloquent Joseph Story.

The duty of selecting and engaging the artists to execute these works was assigned to a Committee of one, as will be seen in the following votes.

" At a meeting of the Trustees of the Proprietors of the Cemetery of Mount Auburn, holden Nov. 6th, 1854, the following votes were passed :—

Voted, That the President be instructed and authorised in the name and behalf of this Corporation, to contract with some suitable artist, to be selected by him, for a statue of *John Winthrop*, in marble, the cost of which shall not exceed five thousand dollars.

Voted, That the President be instructed and authorised in the name and behalf of this Corporation, to contract with some suitable artist, to be selected by him, for a statue of *James Otis*, in marble, the cost of which shall not exceed five thousand dollars.

Voted, That the President be instructed and authorised, in the name and behalf of this Corporation, to contract with some suitable artist, to be selected by him, for a statue of *John Adams*, in marble, the cost of which shall not exceed five thousand dollars.

Attest,

HENRY M. PARKER, *Secretary.*"

In pursuance of the above votes, artists were immediately selected, and contracts signed for the execution of the statues. Considerable progress was made, and as the work advanced, parts of the stipulated price were paid as they became due. In this stage of the business, Mr. Nazro, at a meeting, April 7th, 1856, proposed an inquiry whether these contracts had gone so far that they could not be rescinded. A Committee, consisting of Messrs. Nazro, Curtis, and Lawrence, were appointed · " to examine, consider, and report whether the aforesaid contracts can be rescinded." At an adjourned meeting, April 21st, this Committee reported adversely to the measure, and a minority report was also made by Mr. Nazro in favor of rescinding. Both reports were ordered to be put on record. On a final vote by yeas and nays, on a motion of Mr. Gould to accept the report of the Committee, the Trustees decided in the affirmative as follows: Yeas, Messrs. Curtis, Gould, Lawrence, and Read ; Nays, Messrs. Crocker, McKean, Nazro, and Tisdale, — the President giving his casting vote in the affirmative. Messrs. Bangs, Cheever, and Little, were absent.

The artists selected for these different works, in pursuance of the votes heretofore stated, were Richard S. Greenough, by whom the statue of Governor Winthrop was finished in Florence, and placed on its pedestal in little more than three years ; — Thomas Crawford, who had modelled, and nearly completed, in Rome, the majestic figure of James Otis, when the untimely death of the pre-eminent sculptor left the work to receive its last finish from other hands ; —

and, lastly, Randolph Rogers, by whom a spirited statue of John Adams was promptly executed, but, unfortunately, lost at sea, on its way from Italy. A duplicate of the statue was immediately undertaken, and finished by Mr. Rogers. These artists are all Americans, — natives of Massachusetts and New York.

At a meeting, Sept. 4th, 1855, the Trustees voted, that the Committee on Lots be authorized to lay out such number of quarter lots, containing seventy-five feet each, and in such places as they may deem expedient, each such quarter lot to be sold for fifty dollars.

April 5th, 1858. The need of a Special Police on the ground having been occasionally felt, Mr. Bangs was appointed a Committee to request the Mayor and Aldermen, of Cambridge, and the Selectmen, of Watertown, to appoint the Superintendent, the Gate-keeper, and two other suitable men, to be nominated by the Superintendent, as Special Policemen in and around the Cemetery of Mount Auburn, without compensation. The Committee reported, May 3d, that this appointment had been made, agreeably to the request.

The water courses in Mount Auburn consisted, originally, of a series of small ponds, apparently

stagnant, but communicating with each other by
filtration through the sand or gravel. In rainy
periods, the water in these ponds stands at different heights ; but, in times of drought, the surfaces
approach more nearly the same level. Formerly, a
continuous flow of water took place from Wyeth's
Meadow, lying north of the main road, across
the road into what is now called the Lawn, and
thence across what is now Central Avenue, into
Garden Pond, — the upper portion of which, next
the avenue, is since filled up. To Garden Pond
there was no outlet ; but the water escaped, by
percolation, through Indian Ridge into Auburn
Lake, formerly Meadow Pond. Twenty years
ago, this beautifully situated little lake was a bog
meadow, covered with grass and bushes. It has
been gradually excavated, without expense, by
the removal of mud, which is mostly composed of
decayed leaves and other decomposed vegetable
substances, and is used to enrich the soil. In
1857, a generous purchase was made by Miss
A. M. Loring, of two thousand feet of land, at
the head of this lake, for $1000, — the land to
be forever kept open for ornamental purposes,
and the money to be expended in repairing and
stoning the edges of this lake. The Trustees,

after expending this sum for the purpose required, proceeded, on the following year, to finish the inclosure in the same style, at the expense of the Corporation. The whole bank is now stoned and sodded; a path is completed round the upper half, and a carriage road round the lower half, crossing the water by a small bridge, designed by Mr. Mann, at its narrowest part.

The "Lawn" was evidently, in former times, a continuation of Wyeth's Meadow. As it is too low for cemetery purposes, an excavation was, at one time, begun, for the purpose of converting it into a lake. But this purpose was changed; and it is now decided to raise the surface one foot, and to cover it with loam and grass, with a view to its being always kept open for ornament, and for affording a prospect of the Chapel from the road.

Living springs exist at the bottom of all the principal ponds, and are seen discharging, whenever the water is drawn off for the purpose of deepening the ponds, or removing the mud. In the course of time, it is probable that most of the smaller ponds will be filled up, and the larger ones contracted, by raising, and symmetrically repairing their banks with edgings of stone.

In this way the small pond, in Consecration Dell, was repaired in 1854, and Forest Pond in 1859. The west end of Garden Pond was filled up with gravel to the height of six and a half feet above the water in 1855 – 6, for the sum, by contract, of $850. The land thus created has been laid out in lots, and a part of these are already sold.

A deep and abrupt hollow, contiguous to the west side of the Chapel, though desirable in situation, had been unsaleable, on account of the character of the surface. The Trustees voted, August 4th, 1856, to cause this hollow to be filled with gravel taken from the bank east of the gate. The land thus made has since been sold at advanced prices, — a part of it for $2 per foot.

A house for the Superintendent had been voted to be made, originally, by repairing an old building, which was found standing within the premises when the land was purchased. Afterwards, Oct. 18th, 1832, a Committee was appointed to erect a cottage for the Superintendent, at an expense not exceeding $2000. A small house and barn were erected, which were used by the Superintendent for more than twenty years. At a meeting of the Trustees, Oct. 1st,

1855, it was voted, that the Committee on
Grounds be authorized to remove this house and
the adjacent buildings from the Cemetery, if
they shall think it expedient. The removal was
accordingly made. A new house for the Superintendent was built on the side of the road
opposite the gate, on a lot of land purchased
by the Trustees a few years before, from Mr.
Rufus Howe, Superintendent. The gravel was
first removed from the surface of this land, and
used, in part, in filling up the west end of
Garden Pond. This house, with the outhouses
and appendages, cost in all about $5000.

For many years after the establishment of the
Cemetery, the office of Gate-keeper was discharged by a laboring man. In 1854, a new
office was created of Superintendent's Clerk, —
which office, since that year, has been held by
the same person who officiates as Gate-keeper.

In 1857, a new By-Law was introduced, providing for the appointment of a GARDENER, who
shall be charged with the care and repairing
of lots for those proprietors who may desire
that service; and who shall keep for sale shrubs,
trees, and flowers, at the Cemetery. Mr. Anthony Apple having been appointed to that office,

a lease was executed to him of the land west of
the Superintendent's house, on which he has
proceeded to erect a green-house, and cultivate a
garden.

The Trustees have, at different times, introduced ornamental trees, and flowering shrubs,
into various parts of the grounds. The last
importation consisted of four or five hundred
Rhododendrons, in the spring of 1859, of which
nearly the whole appear flourishing, and in
vigorous condition. A great variety of shrubs
and flowers, native and exotic, are cultivated by
proprietors themselves about their respective lots.

STONE FARM.

It has long been thought desirable that the
Corporation should possess the estate called, on
the map, " The Stone Farm," containing about
sixteen acres, occupying the whole space between
the southern boundary of Mount Auburn and the
southerly part of Coolidge Avenue. This lot, also,
surrounded and cut off from the Cemetery a gore
of two or three acres, already owned by the Corporation, and which could only be made available

when the intervening land should be procured.
A negotiation was undertaken by Mr. Little, one
of the Board of Trustees; and, at a meeting
April 3d, 1854, a letter was read from Mr. J. B.
Dana, of Cambridge, addressed to Mr. Little, as
one of the Trustees, offering to sell this estate
to the Corporation, on conditions therein named.
After due consideration, it was unanimously
voted, "That it is expedient for this Corporation to purchase the Stone Estate, now owned
and offered to this Board by J. B. Dana, Esq.,
and adjoining Mount Auburn, on the southerly
side, containing about sixteen acres, more or less,
with the buildings thereon; and that the President, with Messrs. Little and Bangs, be a
Committee, with full power, to carry this vote
into effect."

At the following meeting, April 22d, the
purchase was reported as being completed, for
the sum of $24,120, on the following valua-
tion : —

16 acres, at $1250, . . .		$20,000
1 rood, $13\frac{8}{10}$ rods, . . .		420
Buildings, per agreement, . .		3,700
		$24,120

The same Committee had been likewise authorised, if they should think it expedient, to negotiate
for certain lands on the westerly side of Mount
Auburn.   On examination, however, they did not
find such purchase to be expedient or desirable.

At a meeting of the Trustees, March 1, 1858,
it was voted — " That the Committee on Grounds
be instructed to expend $1000 per annum, in
grading, and improving the unsold parts of the
land within the Cemetery, and that the earth
removed by this process be applied towards
filling up the superfluous ponds and hollows in
the grounds."   This provision, if kept up for a
few years, will gradually and imperceptibly effect
the desired changes, without subjecting the Corporation to any sudden or inconvenient expenditure.

July 6th, 1858.   A communication having been
received from Mr. Lawrence, Treasurer of Harvard College, in regard to some encroachments
in the boundary line between the land of the
two Corporations, Mr. Gould was made a Committee, with full power, to settle the same.   A
report of a satisfactory adjustment, by a little
variation of the boundary, was reported by that
gentleman, at a subsequent meeting.

May 4th, 1859. In consequence of the decease of Mr. Bangs, one of the Board of Trustees, Mr. Curtis presented the following Resolutions, which were unanimously adopted : —

" Whereas, By the decease of the late Isaiah Bangs, Esq., the Proprietors of the Cemetery of Mount Auburn have been deprived of the services of a faithful officer, who, during five years, devoted himself to their interests with a zeal and fidelity rarely equalled.

And whereas the Board of Trustees have lost a companion, whose good temper, amenity, and candor were conspicuous in all his relations with them, —

It is voted, that the Board of Trustees desire to express the sense they entertain of the lost which they and the Proprietors of Mount Auburn have sustained by the death of their late friend and fellow Trustee.

Voted, That a copy of the foregoing Preamble and Vote be sent by the Secretary to the family of Mr. Bangs."

In the summer of 1859, a marble statue of the late Hosea Ballou, an eminent Minister of the Universalist Church in Boston, executed by Mr. E. A. Brackett, sculptor, of Boston, was erected

6

by a subscription of his parishioners and friends
on the east side of Central Avenue.

Mr. Gould, one of the Board of Trustees,
died, Oct. 24th, 1859, having been in office for
twenty-seven years.   At the next meeting, Nov.
7th, the following Resolutions were unanimously
adopted : —

" The Trustees of Mount Auburn Cemetery
are deeply impressed by the act of Providence
which has taken from them one of the oldest,
most faithful, and most esteemed of their number.

They hold in grateful remembrance the long
and friendly intercourse by which he has co-
operated with them in the care of a solemn
public trust, and the fidelity, zeal, and undeviating
good temper with which he has applied himself
to the discharge of this duty.

They recollect, with unmixed satisfaction, the
disinterested and honorable character of their
friend; his blameless life ; his warm and generous
instincts; the unalterable integrity with which
he obeyed the promptings of a kind heart,
controlled and guided by a strong judgment
and conscientious love of right.

To the family of the deceased they would convey the expression of their deep-felt sympathy,

in aid of the higher consolation which will always remain to them in contemplating the example of his life, and in cherishing his unspotted memory."

PERMANENT FUND.

A design has been entertained, and repeatedly announced, that, as soon as the large, primary works should have been completed, the Corporation should commence the accumulation of a fund, the prospective income of which should defray the expenses of the Cemetery, after the revenue from the annual sales of land shall have ceased.

In promotion of this object, at a meeting, April 7th, 1856, Mr. Curtis made a communication to the effect that " a plan should be devised whereby a fund might be gradually raised, set apart, and studiously protected, for the purpose of furnishing the means of hereafter defraying the ordinary expenses of the establishment, and to secure the perpetual repair of the ground of the Cemetery." Whereupon, it was voted, that a Committee of three be chosen to consider the expediency of adopting such plan, and to report thereon at a future meeting. Messrs. Curtis, Little, and Nazro, were appointed to constitute this Committee. At a meeting in January, 1857, a majority Report was submitted by the two first named gentlemen only, and was adopted by the Trustees.

At the meeting in February following, the whole subject was re-opened for the purpose of making some more effectual provision to ensure the safety of said fund, and was referred to the same Committee, in the following terms: — "To consider and report upon a plan for securing the preservation and continuance of the fund which has been ordered to be established, for the perpetual care and preservation of the Cemetery and its appurtenances; and also to report such regulations for the investment and use of the said fund as they may deem expedient."

A Report, with the Orders accompanying, was presented by a majority of the Committee, April 6th, 1857, and, on the same day, was adopted by the Board of Trustees, and is as follows: —

" The undersigned, the majority of the Committee appointed to report a plan for ensuring the preservation and continuance of the accumulating fund, have considered the subject, and ask leave to Report: —

That they find that the establishment of the said fund is an act generally received with favor

by the proprietors whom they have conferred
with; and they have no doubt that it will be
universally approved, when it is known that by
it the future prosperity of the Cemetery will be
secured. With a view to this end, your Committee have taken into consideration the means
of securing the *perpetual preservation* of this
safety fund; and, after consulting some of the
most sagacious proprietors, they have come to
the conclusion to recommend the adoption of an
order by the Trustees, — that, in all the deeds
of lots which shall hereafter be issued, there
be inserted a covenant, that this fund shall
be increased, by yearly additions, and by the
accumulation of the interest, until it reaches the
sum of one hundred and fifty thousand dollars;
when the interest, and that alone, may be applied,
if the wants of the Corporation require it, to
the payment of the expenses of the Cemetery. If
the Trustees in office at that time shall not need
the income of this fund for expenses, they can, if
they see fit, permit it to accumulate still longer.

In order to carry this design into effect, it will
be expedient to amend the proposition adopted
January 5th, 1857, by providing that, instead
of placing the income at the disposal of the

officers, at the end of *twenty* years, it shall not be made use of until the accumulated capital shall amount to the sum before mentioned, namely, one hundred and fifty thousand dollars.

With these views, your Committee recommend the passage of the following Orders.

CHARLES P. CURTIS,
CHARLES C. LITTLE.

It is ordered, by the Trustees of the Cemetery of Mount Auburn, that, in the month of December of each year, the Treasurer of the Proprietors of the Cemetery of Mount Auburn shall deposit with the Massachusetts Hospital Life Insurance Company, if they will receive it on as favorable conditions as other deposits, in trust for the said Proprietors, a sum equal to one *fifth* part of the gross proceeds of the lots, and parts of lots, and intermediate spaces between lots, which shall have been sold subsequently to the first day of December, in the year preceding; the interest of which sums shall, annually or oftener, be added to the capital, for the purpose, and upon the principle, of accumulation, until the whole of said deposits, with the accumulated interest, shall amount to one hundred and fifty thousand dollars.

And, when the said sum shall have amounted to the sum of one hundred and fifty thousand dollars, it shall be lawful for the Trustees, if they see fit, to withdraw the income thereof, and appropriate the same to the care, preservation, and keeping in order of the Cemetery and its appurtenances, to the payment of the salaries, and to the other necessary expenses of the institution ; and, by vote of *four fifths* of the Trustees for the time being, they may withdraw, from time to time, the principal of the said fund, and invest the same as hereinafter is prescribed.

If, at any time, the Trustees shall deem the Massachusetts Hospital Life Insurance Company to be an *unsafe place of deposit* of the said fund, and shall by a vote of a majority of all the members of the Board, so declare of record, the said fund may be withdrawn from the custody of the said Insurance Company, as soon as by the conditions of the deposit it may be, and shall then be, invested in the name of the Proprietors of the Cemetery of Mount Auburn, upon the same trusts, in the public debt of the United States, or in that of the State of Massachusetts, or in the debt of the City of Boston, or the City of Charlestown, or the City of Roxbury, or the

City of Cambridge, or in mortgages of real estate in Boston : provided that no mortgage shall be taken for a sum exceeding two thirds of the value of the estate as it stands, when taken, on the valuation books of the assessors of the city taxes; nor for a period exceeding five years; nor in which the interest shall not be payable as often as annually; to which shall be added insurance against fire by some competent insurance company in Boston, for the amount of the loan, or such proportion thereof as the value of the buildings on the land shall enable the owner to obtain ; which insurance shall be renewed, from time to time, at the expense of the mortgagor and his assigns, and shall be payable, in case of loss, to the Trustees of the Cemetery of Mount Auburn.

It is ordered, that in all the deeds which shall hereafter be issued, to the purchasers of lots, parts of lots, or other parcels of land in the Cemetery, the following covenant shall be inserted : —

' And the said Proprietors of the Cemetery of Mount Auburn further covenant to and with the said   heirs and assigns, that the Provisions of an order passed by the Trustees of this Corporation, on the sixth day of April. in the year eighteen hundred and fifty-seven (which is made part of this covenant, as if herein repeated), for the establishment and security of a fund for the preservation of the Cemetery and its appurtenances, shall be forever kept, observed, and performed by the said Corporation.' "

The permanent fund thus instituted is already in a state of prosperous growth, in the third year of its accretion, and without inconvenience to the Corporation. Its present rate of accumulation is about $5000 per year, and this ratio may be expected regularly to increase with the accumulation of interest.

ANNUAL REPORTS.

——◆——

The remaining History of Mount Auburn Cemetery will be learnt from the following cotemporaneous reports of the last four years:—

ANNUAL REPORT OF THE TRUSTEES OF THE MOUNT AUBURN CEMETERY, READ TO THE PROPRIETORS AT THEIR MEETING IN JANUARY, 1856.

Previously to 1856, the Annual Report, required by the Act of Incorporation, had, in most cases, been made orally by the President at the yearly meeting of the Proprietors. Of late years the increased interest manifested by the Proprietors in the affairs of the Cemetery, has called for the reading and subsequent printing of this Report.

THE Trustees of Mount Auburn Cemetery are gratified in being able to report that the property of the Corporation remains as heretofore, in a secure and satisfactory state.

A considerable sum has been expended during the last year, in repairing, grading, and paving at the sides, some of the principal avenues. Many of the superfluous trees have been removed, and the branches of others trimmed away, so that the whole ground has a more finished and ornamental appearance than it before possessed. Much remains still to be done in the judicious and careful prosecution of these and similar improvements.

The westerly portion of Garden Pond, near Central Avenue, has justly been considered a blemish to Mount Auburn, on account of the stagnant condition of the water, and the muddiness of the banks and bottom. A contract has been made for filling up this pond with gravel from the neighboring hill, for the sum of $ 850. The earth will be raised about six and a half feet above the present surface of the water, by which operation the Corporation will gain more than an acre of valuable land in one of the most eligible parts of the Cemetery.

Some preparatory arrangements have been made for the occupation of the Stone Farm purchased last year by the Trustees. The principal avenues have been prospectively surveyed and planted with young trees at suitable distances. Nearly the whole of these trees were in healthy condition at the end of the summer.

The Chapel has been taken down as far as the base course, and rebuilt during the past season, in a strong and durable manner. The blemished and insufficient stones inserted by the unfaithfulness of the contractors, have been replaced with others of proper size and appearance, and the character of the building is now in all respects satisfactory as to strength, solidity, and durability. No change has been made in the design except by the introduction of some additional ornament outside. The interior walls not being sufficiently dry, the painting is deferred till next season.

The Statues intended to occupy the interior of the Chapel are all in progress, under contracts made with artists of high eminence in their profession. The statue of Gov. Winthrop is to be executed by Richard Greenough, — that of James Otis by Thomas Crawford, — that of John Adams by Randolph Rogers, — that of Judge Story is by William W. Story. The model statuettes of the first and third of these, are already completed, — that of the second is promised soon, while the fourth statue is already finished and in possession of the Trustees.

A vote has passed the Trustees for laying out quarter lots of seventy-five square feet each, and offering them for sale at $50 each. This will accommodate a certain class of purchasers who have occasion for but small space, and at the same time will enhance the product of the land sold.

The late Superintendent, Mr. Rufus Howe, having resigned his office, the Trustees have elected Mr. Jonathan Mann to fill the vacancy. This election, however, is temporary, and subject to future confirmation.

An application has been made to the Trustees by a large and influential body of the proprietors, in favor of building a Conservatory for the benefit of those persons who may wish to obtain plants or flowers upon the spot. The subject has received consideration, and is referred to the next Board of Trustees.

It will be seen by the Treasurer's Report that the expenditures of the last year have considerably exceeded those of any preceding year. This is in part owing to the payments which have become due on certain large operations, such as are not likely to recur, and partly to the state of transition between the retirement of the former Superintendent and the introduction of his successor. The Trustees entertain the hope that a more economical system of labor will be introduced, and that the necessary work on the grounds will be performed by a smaller number of hands than heretofore.

A great number of outstanding accounts for work done by order of individuals, in different lots of the

Cemetery, had remained uncollected by the late
Superintendent, until they were found to amount
in the aggregate to about $5000.   Immediate
measures have been taken to collect these dues
as far as possible, and about $2500 have already
been received by the Treasurer.   It is hoped
that a large portion of the remainder may yet
be saved to the Corporation.

The future security of Mount Auburn will
depend on the fidelity and economy with which its
affairs are administered, and with which its prospective plans are carried out as contemplated by
its founders.   It may be assumed that all the large
and more expensive operations which have been
kept in view since the foundation of the establishment, are now either paid or provided for.   It only
remains, by a judicious and careful management of
expenditures, to keep the Cemetery in suitable
repair, and at the same time to accumulate a fund
for its perpetual preservation.   Both these objects
can easily be accomplished by the exercise of a
common degree of discretion and economy in the
management of the receipts and funds.   But on
the other hand, they will assuredly be defeated, if
hereafter, either by reckless expenditures or by
improper appropriations, the steady accretion of
a reserved fund should be prevented.

As nearly as it can now be estimated, the eventual value of the unsold land at Mount Auburn may be assumed at about $300,000, at present prices. The current expenses of the Cemetery may be assumed at $10,000 per annum. On this approximate calculation, if the whole of the unsold land should be disposed of in ten years, there would remain a balance of $200,000, without including interest. But on the other hand, if it should take thirty years to sell the land, then the whole proceeds would be absorbed by the current expenses, and not a dollar from these receipts would be left for the future support of the establishment.

It must be obvious to the proprietors, as it has been to the Trustees, that the only safety against the ultimate impoverishment and decay of the Cemetery must consist in a rigid determination on the part of future Boards who may be entrusted with the management of this property, to reserve annually, such a sum from the receipts of the current year, whether those receipts be larger or smaller, as shall insure the steady increase of the permanent fund, and the eventual realization of sufficient invested property to keep the Cemetery in perpetual repair after the sale of the land shall have been completed.

It is in the power of every proprietor to promote the interest and increase the income of the Corporation, in the following ways : —

1. By employing none but the workmen belonging to the place, for the execution of labor and the repairing of lots. A circular on this subject has already been addressed to the proprietors.

2. By introducing new proprietors or otherwise promoting the sale of lots. If each proprietor should introduce a new proprietor, the establishment would at once be placed on a footing of entire independence.

Mount Auburn, in most respects, takes precedence of other cemeteries which have been founded in imitation of it. The peculiar character of its natural features had attracted attention long before its purchase, and the surrounding landscape now seen from the top of its highest edifice, is unsurpassed in natural and cultivated beauty. It exceeds all similar establishments in this country in the size and durability of its larger constructions, and is about to lead, instead of following them, in the interest of its historic and monumental sculptures. As it is not probable that the present boundaries can ever be much enlarged, and as the lots are being steadily taken up at increasing prices, so that the map of the ground already appears covered with them, we may anticipate that the time is not very remote, when the value of these lots will be best known by the difficulty of obtaining them.

By order of the Trustees.

JACOB BIGELOW, *President.*

ANNUAL REPORT OF THE TRUSTEES OF THE MOUNT AUBURN CEMETERY, JANUARY, 1857.

THE Cemetery of Mount Auburn continues in a safe and improving condition, not less than it has done in all the previous years of its history. During the past season, some new works of small magnitude have been undertaken, and some large ones previously begun have been carried to completion.

The upper end of Garden Pond (a pool of stagnant muddy water) has been filled up to the height of about six feet above its former surface, with gravel taken from the hill near the gate. A large

7

stone drain is laid through the centre, over which, for economy of space, an avenue will be laid out. The greater portion of the hill has been levelled. Garden Avenue has been moved nearer to the fence. A part of the trees on its border have been transplanted to the south side, and the whole re-arranged with reference to their good appearance and room for future growth. A hollow near Alder Path, and one south-westerly of the Chapel, have also been filled up. By these measures collec-tively, about two acres of valuable land in the most eligible parts of the Cemetery have been redeemed, at an expense many times less than their present value.

The old house occupied by the Superintendent, together with its outhouses, have been removed, and a new house for the Superintendent has been built on land owned by the Corporation, outside and easterly of the gate. This building (designed by Mr. H. W. Hartwell) has been constructed in a substantial and durable manner, at an expense of about four thousand dollars.*

The area in front of the Chapel has been en-

---

* A stable, fences, and other appurtenances were afterward added, increasing the cost about $1000. The stable was built in 1859.

larged, by the purchase and removal of several lots which were formerly situated on the same space. It is justly considered important to the good appearance of the principal edifices, such as the Tower, the Chapel, and the Gate, that no inferior structures should be placed so near them, as to interfere with, or impair their isolated effect.

The Chapel has been completed in a satisfactory manner, both as to appearance and durability. Two of the pedestals and one of the statues, destined for the interior, are already in their places. The three remaining statues are understood to be in a state of forwardness, and may be expected to arrive here in from one to two years.

Due attention has been paid to repairing and improving the avenues and paths, and to extending the pavement of gutters where it was thought necessary. Some expense has been incurred in repairing the damage done by the heavy rains of the last summer.

The thinning out and trimming of trees has been in gradual progress, under the superintendence of Mr. Mann, the present able and active Superintendent, with whose economy and skill as a landscape gardener, the Trustees have great reason to be satisfied.

The names of some of the persons interred in the public lots, having been lost through the inattention of their relatives and friends, measures have been taken, as far as possible, to identify these persons, and, in future, to remedy such neglect, by affixing to each grave a number on stone, with a corresponding number of reference on the Superintendent's books.

An important vote has passed the Trustees, providing that the land left vacant as intermediate space between lots, and not exceeding ten feet in width between any two lots, may be sold to the nearest lot holder or holders, at one third of the selling price per foot, at the time of such sale, with the condition that the said land shall forever be kept open, and without interments.   The advantage of this arrangement consists not only in the probable increase of the funds of the Corporation from the expected sales, but also in the opportunity afforded to lot owners who may wish to avail themselves of it, to protect their lots, at a small expense, against the eventual occupation of these spaces for small lots or single interments — a thing which the experience of older cemeteries has shown to be very likely to happen.

The comparative smallness of this year's balance

of stocks, cash, and debts receivable, remaining in the Treasurer's hands, is not an index of the true pecuniary position of Mount Auburn. It will be seen that the purchase of the Stone Farm, the making of land within the Cemetery, and the erection of the Superintendent's house, are not expenditures but investments — a conversion of more precarious stocks into real property at the Cemetery, much more certain hereafter to yield an abundant return, than any of the funds which have been converted for their purchase. It may be safely assumed, that the financial position of Mount Auburn was never so strong, nor its preservation and embellishments so satisfactory to its proprietors, nor so attractive to purchasers, as they will be found to be at the expiration of the coming year.

In conformity with the intention which has been repeatedly announced, the Trustees have this year voted to commence the accumulation of a permanent fund for the future preservation of the Cemetery, after all the land shall have been sold. A report of a Committee has been adopted providing for the deposit annually, under certain circumstances, of one fifth part of the gross proceeds of the sales of lots, with the Massachusetts Hospital Life Insurance Company, to accumulate at compound interest for the term of twenty years. Should the receipts and necessary expenditures continue about the same as they now are, and should the same conservative policy which has hitherto governed the Trustees continue to be observed by them, there is no doubt that an ample permanent fund will have been accumulated for the perpetual care and preservation of the Cemetery, after all the land shall have been disposed of.

A new Catalogue has been ordered to be printed for the use of the Proprietors, which is enlarged and corrected up to the present time.

A code of By-Laws, not before published, has now been added, consisting of extracts from the recorded standing votes of the Trustees, amended and considerably enlarged.

Respectfully submitted,

In behalf of the Trustees.

JACOB BIGELOW, *President.*

ANNUAL REPORT OF THE TRUSTEES OF THE
MOUNT AUBURN CEMETERY, JANUARY, 1858.

SINCE the last Annual Meeting a new and
complete Catalogue of the Proprietors of Mount
Auburn Cemetery has been published, having
been corrected from former editions with much
labor and care on the part of the Secretary.
To this Catalogue has been prefixed a code of
By-Laws, compiled and digested from the standing
votes of the Trustees, with such amendments as
were considered necessary.

Since the adoption of this code, it has been
found that the duties therein required of the
Superintendent were too onerous and diversified
to be properly performed by one individual. A
new office has therefore been created, and a new
By-Law introduced, providing for the appointment, and prescribing the duties and powers of
a *Gardener* to the Cemetery. The person so
appointed is to take charge of, and keep in repair,
the lots of such proprietors as may apply to him
for that service, and on such terms as may be
agreed on between the parties ; he is also to keep
for sale, at some convenient place designated by

the Trustees, shrubs, trees, and flowers, and be
ready to furnish, plant, or cultivate the same at
his own expense, and at such price and remuneration as may be agreed on with the purchasers.
This plan, which costs nothing to the Corporation,
has been found to work well in other cemeteries
where it has been tried.

The Trustees have appointed to this office Mr.
Anthony Apple, an experienced gardener, and
have leased to him a piece of ground nearly
opposite the Gate, on which he has erected a
conservatory and commenced a garden. The
destruction of his first green-house, by fire, and
the consequent expense of rebuilding it, entitles
him to the charitable consideration of those who
may be likely to need his services.

The experiment made last year of transplanting
some dozens of large trees in the neighborhood
of the Gate, has proved eminently successful, not
one of them having been lost or injured by the
operation. A somewhat similar alteration is now
in progress on the westerly side of the Gate.

By the liberality of one of the proprietors, the
sum of one thousand dollars has been expended
in grading, stoning, and otherwise improving the
border of Meadow Pond. An open space of two

thousand square feet, inclosing the fountain at the head of the pond, is to be forever kept open for ornamental purposes. It is hoped that other proprietors may be induced to follow so praise-worthy an example. The Trustees have voted to appropriate to a similar repair of Forest Pond, all sums which may be derived from the sale of intermediate spaces between lots bordering on this pond. Some of the abuttors have already subscribed to this object, and it is believed that others will be disposed to promote an object bene-ficial to themselves and to the Corporation.

The statues expected from Italy, and intended to decorate the interior of the Chapel, have not yet arrived. That of Governor Winthrop, by Mr. Greenough, is announced as completed in Florence, and may be expected here in the Spring or sooner. Mr. Crawford's statue of James Otis has been unhappily delayed by the death of that distinguished and lamented artist. Letters from his representatives, however, express the belief that it is already completed in Rome, and will be forwarded in the course of the Spring. The fourth statue, that of John Adams, was shipped from Leghorn about the first of September, in the Oxford, a vessel reported as deserted at sea, and probably lost. The amount which would have been due on the delivery of this statue, was insured by the sculptor, Mr. Rogers, who is confident of being able to execute a duplicate from the model in the course of another year. When these works are completed, and in their places, the Corporation will have acquired a valuable and most appropriate embellishment, giving them precedence over all other cemeteries in this country, at an expense not exceeding three per cent. of the estimated gross outlay of Mount Auburn, or six per cent. of the expenditures up to the present time.

Among the auspicious events of the last year is the commencement of a permanent fund, provided for the support and preservation of the Cemetery, after the receipts from land sales shall have ceased. A first instalment of three thousand five hundred and ten dollars has been paid by the Treasurer to the Massachusetts Hospital Life Insurance Company, in pursuance of a vote of the Trustees, by which it is required that one fifth part of the gross proceeds of sales of land shall be annually deposited with said company, until the whole sum thus deposited, together with its accumulations of interest, shall amount to one hundred and fifty thousand dollars. The farther to insure the stability of this investment, the Trustees have caused to be inserted in every new deed of conveyance a covenant binding the Corporation to the preservation and increase of this permanent fund, so that no future Board of Trustees will have the power to misapply or to divert any part of it from its legitimate destination.

By the Treasurer's Report it will be seen that the receipts of the last year have considerably exceeded those of the previous year, while the expenditures have been less; showing that the Trustees have thus far been able to keep up the same prudent policy which has heretofore governed their movements.

For the Trustees.

JACOB BIGELOW, *President.*

Boston, February 1st, 1858.

ANNUAL REPORT OF THE TRUSTEES OF THE MOUNT
AUBURN CEMETERY, JANUARY, 1859.

IN 1831 the Massachusetts Horticultural Society
purchased the tract of land since inclosed and
known as the Cemetery of Mount Auburn. The
principal part of this land was first conditionally
engaged for a Cemetery by the Corresponding
Secretary of the Society, and the purchase was not
completed until one hundred individual subscribers
for burial lots had been obtained from the community at large, and thus a sufficient sum insured to
compensate the Society for its outlay.

It was at first intended to divide the land purchased into two parts — the one to be occupied as
a cemetery, and the other as an experimental garden for horticultural purposes. But in a few
years it became apparent that the proposed garden
was not likely to be wanted, and in 1835, under
an Act of the Legislature, the Horticultural
Society conveyed the whole land known as Mount
Auburn to a new Corporation, entitled " The
Proprietors of the Cemetery of Mount Auburn."
By the terms of this conveyance, the new Corporation was to pay annually to the Horticultural

Society one fourth part of the proceeds of the sales of lots, after deducting fourteen hundred dollars, which last sum was intended for the defrayment of annual expenses.   In this way things remained until 1858.

In the meanwhile the Proprietors of Mount Auburn had, at sundry times, made additional purchases of land in the neighborhood of their Cemetery — the greatest of which is that of the estate known as the " Stone Farm," on the southerly side of Mount Auburn ; and various questions have arisen, both before and since that purchase, as to the right of the Horticultural Society to participate in the results of such purchases ; also to the claim of that Society for a part of the proceeds of interments made in " public lots," the fee of which is still in the Corporation of Mount Auburn ; also in regard to the expense of filling up and grading ponds and useless pieces of land so as to render them available for cemetery purposes ; and also in regard to various other unsettled matters.

With a view to the final adjustment of these and any other questions which might remain, the Trustees of Mount Auburn Cemetery, during the last year, appointed a Committee of Conference, to meet

a similar Committee to be appointed on the part of
the Horticultural Society, and to report terms of
agreement which might be satisfactory to both
parties.   The Committee of the Proprietors of
Mount Auburn, consisting of Messrs. Bigelow,
Gould and Cheever, were met by a Committee of
the Horticultural Society, consisting of Messrs.
Stickney, Wilder, Rand, Walker, Austin, and
Hovey, and a report was agreed on, which was
afterwards unanimously accepted by both parties
in interest, and by them carried into effect.   An
Indenture of two parts has been duly executed by
the two Corporations, under which the parties
covenant and agree with each other in the manner
following : —

"First.   That the said Cemetery as now existing, and situated south of the street called Mount
Auburn Street, in Cambridge, together with the
lands already purchased as an enlargement thereof,
and all additions which shall hereafter be made to
the same, shall be held by the said Proprietors,
and the entire control, management, and direction
of the same, and of all works and improvements
therein, and expenditures thereon, shall be and
remain in the said Proprietors and their officers,

in as full and complete a manner as the same are now vested in and entrusted to them by Act of Legislature incorporating the said Proprietors, passed on the thirty-first day of March, A. D. eighteen hundred and thirty-five.

Second. The yearly proceeds of all sales of lands in the said Cemetery as it now exists, or may hereafter be enlarged, together with all amounts received for single interments in any public lots or receiving tombs, after the deduction of fourteen hundred dollars therefrom to be retained by the said Proprietors for the purposes stated in said Act, shall, on the first Monday in every year, be divided between the said Proprietors and the said Horticultural Society, according to the terms of the said Act, in following proportions, viz: three fourths to the said Proprietors, and one fourth to the said Society ; and the said Proprietors shall, at such time, render to the said Society a just and true account of all sales made, and of all moneys received by them for such lands and interments during the preceding year, and shall furnish all such vouchers and evidence in regard to the same as the said Society may reasonably require.

Third. The sum of nine thousand eight and $\frac{49}{100}$ dollars, which on the first day of January next

will be due and owing from the said Horticultural
Society to the said Proprietors, shall be paid in
manner following, viz.: The said Proprietors
shall have the right to retain out of the amount
which under the provisions of the preceding Article, will yearly, and in each year, be due and
payable to the said Society, one full half part
thereof of the amount so payable, which part so
retained shall be applied — first, to the payment
of the yearly interest on the said sum, or on such
part as shall remain unpaid, and the residue to the
reduction and final extinguishment of the said
debt, until the same shall be fully paid and discharged; provided, however, that the said Society
shall have the right to pay the whole, or any part
of the said sum at any time.

Fourth. The said Society hereby covenants
with the said Proprietors, that whenever the said
Proprietors shall enclose the lands already purchased in a manner corresponding with the present
Cemetery, or otherwise, as they shall see fit, they
will pay to the said Proprietors one fourth part of
the cost thereof; and in like manner, in case of
any future additions to and enlargements of the
Cemetery, they will pay to the said Proprietors
one fourth part of the cost of enclosing the same,

whenever such enclosure shall be completed —
the time and making such enclosure to be at the
discretion of the said Proprietors.

Fifth. Whenever lands, otherwise unsaleable,
or unfit for purposes of burial, shall be filled up
and improved, the cost of such filling up and im
provement shall first be deducted from the proceeds
of sales of such lands ; and the residue only shall
be the amount to be accounted for by the said
Proprietors, and to be divided between the two
Corporations in the manner specified in the Second
Article of this Indenture ; provided, however, that
the amount of such residue shall never be less than
fifty cents per square foot — except that intermediate spaces between lots, when not intended for
burial, may be sold for sixteen and two thirds cents
per square foot.

Sixth. In case the said Proprietors shall hereafter build Receiving Tombs, Catacombs, or Columbaria, in the said Cemetery, the said Horticultural
Society shall pay one fourth part of the cost
thereof; and shall be entitled to one fourth part
of all amounts received for interments therein.

Seventh. The said Horticultural Society hereby release the said Proprietors from all claims
and demands for or on account of any and all

8

moneys received, or which shall be received, by the said Proprietors for single interments in the said Cemetery prior to the first of January next.

Eighth. It is understood and agreed that the said Horticultural Society have no interest in the lands situated on the northerly side of Mount Auburn Street, on which the Gardener's House now stands, and the said Society hereby expressly disclaims all right and title and interest therein."

It will be seen by the foregoing extracts that the Horticultural Society pay to the Proprietors of the Cemetery the sum of 9008 dollars 49 cents, this being the balance which would be due on the estimated cost, interest and present value of one fourth part of the lands newly purchased, after deducting the necessary off-sets. And the Society farther agrees to pay one fourth part of the expense of an iron fence, &c., round the newly acquired land whenever the same shall be erected. On the other hand, the Proprietors of Mount Auburn agree to place the new lands on the same footing as the old Cemetery, and to pay to the Horticultural Society one fourth part of the proceeds of all sales of these lands after the usual deduction has been made.

The other unsettled questions have been adjusted

in a spirit of compromise and mutual concession, and are believed to be equitable, and entirely satisfactory to both parties.

Since the last Annual Meeting, two of the historic statues, destined for the interior of the Chapel, have arrived from Italy, and are now on their pedestals. These are the statues of Governor Winthrop, by R. S. Greenough, and of James Otis, by Crawford. The fourth statue, that of John Adams, having been lost at sea, a duplicate has been undertaken by the artist, Mr. Rogers, and is promised to arrive in the course of the coming Spring. The execution, and acquisition of these appropriate works of art, are alike creditable to the Corporation, and to the eminent sculptors by whom they have been formed.

The repairing and edging with stone, of Auburn Lake (formerly Meadow Pond) has been completed, and an avenue made round its lower half, crossing the middle of the lake by a handsome bridge, passable for carriages. A corresponding improvement, in stoning up the border of Forest Pond, is in contemplation for the next season. Improvements in grading avenues and moving trees west of the gate have been made, and others are in progress, together with the extension of sundry drains, and the completion of new paths in different parts of the ground. The Trustees have voted to expend one thousand dollars annually in the gradual filling, reclaiming, and improving of sunken lands, which have a prospective value.

The tract of unoccupied ground in the front of the Cemetery, between Garden Pond and the road, constituting one of the most desirable parts of Mount Auburn, is in process of being surveyed, and the lots will be offered for sale early in the Spring.

The Trustees have voted that lots for tombs on the hill-sides, in such places as the Committee on Lots shall approve, may be sold at fifty cents per square foot, on the purchasers binding themselves to erect no tomb or repository which shall not be made air-tight, to the satisfaction of the Committee on Lots.

By the Treasurer's Report it will be seen that the financial affairs of the Corporation are in a safe and prosperous condition. The sales of land during the last year have amounted to $24,434.65, exceeding those of the previous year by $3836. The Permanent Fund for the future preservation of the Cemetery, which was auspiciously commenced last year, has been this year increased by

$5678, making the present total amount of that fund, $9390.33. Besides which the Corporation have always a large reserve beyond their liabilities, more than adequate to meet all anticipated expenses.

In behalf of the Trustees,

JACOB BIGELOW, *President.*

CAUTIONARY SUGGESTIONS.

THE experience of nearly thirty years which have elapsed since the foundation of Mount Auburn, has furnished useful instruction in regard to the management and safe preservation of this public trust in time to come. Its record may also yield profitable information for other establishments which may hereafter be founded on its example. Considered in regard to its success, and the rapid growth which has followed its original movement, Mount Auburn has surpassed the expectations of the most sanguine of its promoters. Yet it is easy to perceive, at this period, that if its progress and extent could have been fully foreseen, various arrangements, both of convenience and economy, could have been more perfectly carried out, and, doubtless, some errors avoided in its management.

The Committee, who were originally charged with the duty of laying out the grounds, made their paths and avenues with reference to the grade of the surface and facility of access to all parts of the Cemetery. The lots, also, were placed for the most part on level spots, and frequently where the purchasers chose to have them, without regard to the economy of the land, or to the size and shape of the intermediate spaces. The experience of late years has induced the Trustees to make both the paths and lots more parallel to each other, and with as little space between them as is consistent with their good appearance. An adherence to this plan hereafter, by preventing waste, will render the unsold land more productive, without in any way injuring the general appearance of the place. Proprietors, however, who may desire to control more land, for use or ornament, can always do so by purchasing it. At present, a space of six feet in front is allowed to every purchaser, between his lot and the avenue or path. And the Trustees have carefully avoided infringing on the intermediate space existing between lots, except when it is unnecessarily large. But it may happen hereafter, that, when all the lots in the Cemetery are sold, some future Board of Trustees may be importuned or tempted to sell these intermediate spaces, as has happened in old cemeteries in Europe and elsewhere. The only perfect security against all such encroachment is for the proprietors to protect themselves, if they see fit, by purchasing the immediate space or border adjoining them, at its present reduced and very small price, as seen in the By-Laws.

The multiplication of trees has already become in Mount Auburn a serious evil. The original wood has apparently more than doubled its boughs and foliage since the beginning of the Cemetery. The ground, as seen from the top of the tower, now looks like a dense, impenetrable forest, in which most of the monuments are concealed from view by the contiguous branches. Where young firs and other evergreens are planted, the level prospect is also wholly intercepted, and the visitor, in many cases, cannot see many rods in advance of his eyes. The Trustees have endeavored in part to abate this evil by thinning out the wood, pruning branches, and cutting away useless trees; and this work is still in gradual progress. But over the trees belonging to individual proprietors, or growing on lots, they have no control, except in obedience to the laws and the wishes of the owners. If application is made to the Superintendent, trees can always be removed without expense to the proprietors.

The custom of continually planting new trees rapidly increases the evil, as will become apparent when the young trees, now set out, shall have attained the age of ten or of fifty years. When trees stand too thickly together, as they do in natural woods, the under branches die for want of sunshine, and are eventually converted into dead limbs or unseemly knots. And, in like manner, the interlocking branches of contiguous trees reciprocally destroy each other, so that when one of a pair is cut down, a hemispherical or half tree remains of the other. Trees planted with reference to their free growth and ultimate good appearance, should not stand nearer than thirty feet, or about two rods apart, — as is seen in the elms and other trees of Boston Mall and Common. Pines, firs, and evergreen trees, except when planted in clumps for ornament, where land is abundant, require still greater distance. When immediate effect is required, young trees may be planted one rod from each other, and, at a subsesequent period, the alternate ones may be removed as soon as they have acquired a height of twenty feet.

The perfection of Mount Auburn, as far as its natural features are concerned, would be attained by diminishing the trees to less than one half of their present number, — leaving broad vistas and open spaces, through which the works of art could be seen ; and the light of the sun might be admitted to the grass and cultivated flowers, to the health of which it is indispensable. Rows of trees are wanted only on the principal avenues, while, in other places, flowers and low flowering shrubs, varied according to the requirements of individual taste, with a few trees left only in unobjectionable places, would greatly improve the picturesque effect of the Cemetery. To purchasers who look forward to the prospective beauty of appearance, the open grounds now existing on the north and south extremes of the Cemetery are more eligible, from their capacity of improvement, than the dense and central parts now occupied by the wood. On such grounds a very few trees are all that can be wanted; and the experience of the last three years has shown that trees twenty and thirty feet high may be transplanted at small expense, and with perfect safety; and such trees may always be had of the Superintendent. But, where trees are already growing on the avenues, a correct taste, and a regard to the future, will probably induce proprietors to introduce only low shrubs and herbaceous plants, and even these with a judicious frugality. As far as good appearance is concerned, the borders of a common lot may contain roses, laurels, and rhododendrons, in moderate numbers, whereas one elm tree is often sufficient for an acre. The pyramidal fir trees which now in some places are cumbersome, from their thickness, should at least have their lower branches trimmed away above the height of the spectator's eye. Many of them ought to be wholly removed.

Common gravel is an article of indispensable use in an establishment like Mount Auburn. Great quantities are required for the making of roads, the grading of lots, and the filling of hollows and ponds. The Trustees, not foreseeing the extraordinary growth and rapid occupation of the land in the Cemetery, have unfortunately sold to applicants, from time to time, the best hills and gravelly knolls within the enclosure. The necessity, therefore, becomes more imperative, that spots containing the remaining sources of supply should not be sold until the gravelly eminences have been first removed for use.

Mount Auburn has been increased at various times until it now covers a space nearly three times as large as Boston Common. This is quite as much as one Superintendent can properly take care of. For the convenient administration of the place hereafter, it may be hoped that future Boards of Trustees will resist the occasional temptation to annex indefinitely such pieces of adjacent land as may be offered to them. Whenever the Cemetery shall be filled, and its permanent fund adequate to defray the expense of its annual support, it is better that new establishments should be created elsewhere, than that Mount Auburn should become unwieldy, and its care difficult, if not impracticable, from its overgrown size. There must be a line at which it will be necessary to stop, and that line has probably been attained already.

The permanent fund is a sacred deposit upon

which alone the institution is to depend for its support after the land shall have been sold. Its only danger to be apprehended is from the cupidity of speculators who, at some future period, may so manage as to obtain temporary control of this fund for improper purposes, — an occurrence not unknown in the financial history of various institutions in our country.

The present Board of Trustees have endeavored to protect this fund by a covenant, giving to every new purchaser a claim on the Corporation for the preservation of the fund entire. This security lasts until the amount of the fund shall have reached one hundred and fifty thousand dollars, when the income may be drawn out and the principal gradually re-invested under certain conditions. It is to be trusted that the Corporation will always elect Trustees who will respect the security, rather than an alleged increase in the productiveness of a fund which is essential and even vital to the support of the establishment after the revenue from the sale of land has ceased.

It has hitherto been the policy of the Trustees to keep on hand a considerable invested surplus, which can be drawn upon in case of emergency, and which, if not wanted, goes to swell by its interest the income of the Corporation. The continual call for repairs, which increases as there are more miles of road to be kept in order, and more rods of fence to be painted or replaced, can only be met by a careful provision of this sort. The present yearly excess of the receipts over the expenditures, even after deducting the amount annually paid to the permanent fund, is amply sufficient for the wants of the establishment. But a large reserve will hereafter be needed to complete the iron fence around the Stone Farm; to replace the western wooden fence when it shall have decayed; to finish the drains and catacombs now in progress; to excavate bogs and build stone borders to lakes, — together with unforeseen exigencies, which, if taken in hand now, would speedily exhaust the whole available capital of the institution. Yet all these improvements will silently and gradually come to pass, without risk or inconvenience, if the Board adhere to their uniform previous policy of not making improvements faster than they are actually wanted and can certainly be paid for.

A good economy will obviously require that

the various structures belonging to the Corporation should be kept in thorough repair. Roofs, windows, paint and pointing of joints, require regular and prompt attention in this respect, for reasons which need no explanation.

The good appearance of buildings depends quite as much upon their site and aspect as upon their intrinsic structure. No edifice can appear to advantage which is covered up or interfered with by others of equal size in its immediate proximity. It is to be hoped that the open spaces now existing about the Tower, the Chapel, and the Gate, will never be encroached on by any subordinate constructions in their immediate neighborhood. It seems not improbable that the Trustees will at some day see the propriety of conveying these spaces in trust, with the condition that they shall forever be kept open, and not occupied as places either for building or interment.

A few suggestions in regard to the occupation and improvement of individual lots will not be superfluous in this place. Mount Auburn was begun under the expectation that single interments in the earth, in separate graves, would take the place of tombs or common receptacles, the tenants of which, it is well known, have but a temporary and precarious occupancy, as these things are usually managed by the remoter friends and successors of the deceased. The following short article, published early in the Daily Advertiser, conveys the sentiments on this subject of the founders of Mount Auburn : —

"It is a part of the original design of this establishment, though not an obligatory one, that interments shall be made in single or separate graves, rather than in tombs. The abundant space afforded by the extensiveness of the tract which has been purchased, precludes the necessity of constructing vaults for the promiscuous concentration of numbers. It is believed that the common grave affords the most simple, natural, and secure method by which the body may return to the bosom of the earth, to be peacefully blended with its original dust. Whatever consolation can be derived from the gathering together of members of the same families, is provided for by the appropriation of lots, each sufficient for a family, while the provision that the same spot or grave shall not be twice occupied for interment, secures to the buried an assurance of undisturbed rest, not always found in more costly constructions.

On the same subject another consideration
may be added. It is desired that the place
may become beautiful, attractive, consoling, —
not gloomy and repulsive, — that what the
earth has once covered it shall not again reveal
to light, — that the resources of art shall not be
wasted in vain efforts to delay or modify the
inevitable courses of nature. It is hoped, therefore, that any sums which individuals may think
it proper to devote to the improvement of the
place of sepulture of themselves and their
friends, may be expended above the surface of
the earth, — not under it. A beautiful monument is interesting to every one. A simple bed
of roses under the broad canopy of heaven, is a
more approachable, a far more soothing object,
than the most costly charnel-house."

Some of the first tombs constructed in the
side hills at Mount Auburn became offensive
from the escape of gas through their upright
iron doors, the crevices of which are never
made permanently tight. On this account, the
Trustees for a time restricted them to the most
distant or outside avenues. Afterwards they
were permitted in places approved by the Trustees, provided they are made in a strong, tight,

and durable manner, and every part, including the door, at least one foot underground. Finally, a vote was passed, Oct. 4th, 1858, "That lots for tombs on the hill sides, in such places as the Committee on Lots shall approve, may be sold at fifty cents per square foot, on the purchasers binding themselves to erect no tomb or repository which shall not be made air tight, to the satisfaction of the Committee on Lots."

The mode of interment now most common at Mount Auburn is that in simple graves, afterwards designated by headstones or some other mark. Where the most permanent security is desired, a separate inclosure of the grave is made of bricks and cement, and afterwards covered with a flat stone. When *tombs* are built, their best construction is found to be that which is in imitation of the ancient *columbaria*, in which a subterranean apartment is provided on one or more sides, with cavities like pigeon holes, the mouths of which are to be tightly closed with bricks and cement, or with a flat stone. The general name of *catacombs* is applied to these at Mount Auburn and at some other places.

9

PART II.

——◆——

ADDRESSES, REPORTS, REGULATIONS, DOCUMENTS, &c.

ADDRESSES, REPORTS, ETC.

"It having been considered important, that the public should be generally informed as.to the character of the two associated establishments, the Hon. EDWARD EVERETT was requested to prepare an Address, explanatory of the objects which it was proposed to accomplish, and he furnished the following, which was published in the Boston papers." — *Horticultural Proceedings,* 1832.

THE PROPOSED RURAL CEMETERY.

AT the late session of the General Court, an Act was passed, enlarging the powers of the Horticultural Society in such a manner, as to enable it to establish a rural cemetery, in connection with the experimental. garden, which forms a part of the original plan of that Society. Preliminary steps have been taken to exercise the powers

granted by this additional act of incorporation.
The subject has been under the consideration of
a large and highly respectable committee, selected
for their known interest in the design ; and a plan
of measures to be pursued, for carrying the object
into effect, has been prepared and adopted.

The spot, which has been selected for this
establishment, has not been chosen without great
deliberation, and a reference to every other place
in the vicinity of Boston, which has been named
for the same purpose. In fact, the difficulty of
finding a proper place has been for several years
the chief obstacle to the execution of this project.
The spot chosen is as near Boston as is consistent
with perfect security from the approach of those
establishments, usually found in the neighborhood
of a large town, but not in harmony with the
character of a place of burial. It stands near a
fine sweep in Charles River. It presents every
variety of surface, rising in one part into a beautiful elevation, level in others, with intermediate
depressions, and a considerable part of the whole
covered with the natural growth of wood. In
fact, the place has long been noted for its rural
beauty, its romantic seclusion, and its fine prospect ; and it is confidently believed, that there is

not another to be named, possessing the same
union of advantages.

It is proposed to set apart a considerable portion
of this delightful spot, for the purpose of a burial
place. Little will be required from the hand of
art to fit it for that purpose. Nature has already
done almost all that is required. Scarcely any
thing is needed but a suitable enclosure, and such
walks as will give access to the different parts of
the enclosed space, and exhibits features to the
greatest advantage. It is proposed, (as it appears
from the report above cited,) to divide the parts
of the tract, best adapted to that purpose, into lots,
containing two hundred or more square feet, to be
used by individuals becoming proprietors of them,
for the purposes of burial. It will be at the option
of those interested, to build tombs of the usual
construction on these lots, or to make graves in
them, when occasion may require ; identifying the
lot by a single monument, or the graves by separate stones, or leaving the whole without any
other ornament than the green turf and the over-
shadowing trees.

By the act of the Legislature, authorizing the
Horticultural Society to establish this Cemetery,
it is placed under the protection of the laws, and

consecrated to the perpetual occupancy of the dead. Being connected with the adjacent experimental garden, it will be under the constant inspection of the Society's Gardener, and thus possess advantages, in reference to the care and neatness with which it will be kept, not usually found in places of burial. A formal act of dedication, with religious solemnities, will impart to it a character of sanctity, and consecrate it to the sacred purposes for which it is destined.

It is a matter of obvious consideration, that, with the rapid increase of the city of Boston, many years cannot elapse, before the deposit of the dead within its limits must cease. It is already attended with considerable difficulty, and is open to serious objections. The establishment now contemplated, presents an opportunity for all, who wish to enjoy it, of providing a place of burial for those, for whom it is their duty to make such provision. The space is ample, affording room for as large a number of lots, as may be required for a considerable length of time; and the price at which they are now to be purchased, it is believed, is considerably less than that of tombs, in the usual places of their construction.

Although no one, whose feelings and principles

are sound, can regard, without tenderness and delicacy, the question, where he will deposit the remains of those, whom it is his duty to follow to their last home, yet it may be feared, that too little thought has been had for the decent aspect of our places of sepulture, or their highest adaptation to their great object. Our burial places are, in the cities, crowded till they are full; nor, in general, does any other object, either in town or country, appear to have been had in view in them, than that of confining the remains of the departed to the smallest portion of earth that will hide them. Trees, whose inexpressible beauty has been provided by the hand of the Creator as the great ornament of the earth, have rarely been planted about our graveyards; the enclosures are generally inadequate and neglected, the graves indecently crowded together, and often, after a few years, disturbed; and the whole appearance as little calculated as possible to invite the visits of the seriously disposed, to tranquillize the feelings of surviving friends, and to gratify that disposition which would lead us to pay respect to their ashes.

Nor has it hitherto been in the power even of those, who might be able and willing to do it, to

remedy these evils, as far as they are themselves
concerned. Great objections exist to a place of
sepulture in a private field; particularly this,
that in a few years it is likely to pass into the
hands of those, who will take no interest in pre-
serving its sacred deposit from the plough. The
mother of Washington lies buried in a field, the
property of a person not related to her family, and
in a spot which cannot now be identified. In the
public graveyard it is not always in the power
of an individual to appropriate to a single place
of burial, space enough for the purposes of decent
and respectful ornament.

The proposed establishment seems to furnish
every facility for gratifying the desire, which must
rank among the purest and strongest of the human
heart, and which would have been much more
frequently indicated, but for the very serious, and
sometimes insuperable obstacles of which we have
spoken. Here it will be in the power of every
one, who may wish it, at an expense considerably
less than that of a common tomb, or a vault
beneath a church, to deposit the mortal remains
of his friends, and to provide a place of burial for
himself, which, while living, he may contemplate
without dread or disgust; one which is secure

from the danger of being encroached upon, as in the graveyards of the city; secluded from every species of uncongenial intrusion; surrounded with everything that can fill the heart with tender and respectful emotions; beneath the shade of a venerable tree, on the slope of the verdant lawn, and within the seclusion of the forest; removed from all the discordant scenes of life.

Such were the places of burial of the ancient nations. In a spot like this were laid the remains of the patriarchs of Israel. In the neighborhood of their great cities the ancient Egyptians established extensive cities of the dead; and the Greeks and Romans erected the monuments of the departed by the road side, on the approach to their cities, or in pleasant groves in their suburbs. A part of the Grove of Academus, near Athens, famous for the school of Plato, was appropriated to the sepulchres of their men of renown; and it was the saying of Themistocles, that the monuments he beheld there would not permit him to sleep. The "Appian Way" was lined with the monuments of the heroes and sages of Rome. In modern times, the Turkish people are eminent for that respectful care of the places of sepulture, which forms an interesting trait of the oriental character. At the head and foot of each grave, a cypress tree is planted, so that the graveyard becomes, in a few years, a deep and shady grove. These sacred precincts are never violated; they form the most beautiful suburbs to the cities, and, not unfrequently, when the city of the living has been swept away by the political vicissitudes, frequent under that government, the Grove of Cypress remains, spreading its sacred shelter over the city of the dead.

In the city of Boston, the inconveniences of the present modes of burial are severely felt; and it is as a becoming appendage and interesting ornament of the town, that this Cemetery should be regarded. When it shall be laid out with suitable walks, and the appropriate spots shall begin to be adorned with the various memorials which affection and respect may erect to the departed, what object in or near Boston will be equally attractive ? What would sooner arrest the attention of the stranger ? Whither would a man of reflection and serious temper sooner direct his steps ? Had such a Cemetery, with prophetic forethought of posterity, been laid out in the first settlement of the country, and all our venerated dead, — the eminent in church and state, — been deposited side by side, with plain but enduring monuments, it would possess already an interest of the most elevated and affecting character. Such a place of deposit is Pere la Chaise, near Paris, which has already become a spot of the greatest interest and attraction, furnishing the model to similar establishments in various parts of Europe, and well deserving to be had in view, in that which is in contemplation here.

The vicinity of our venerable University suggests an interesting train of associations, connected with this spot. It has ever been the favorite resort of the students. There are hundreds now living, who have passed some of the happiest hours of the happiest period of their lives, beneath the shade of the trees in this secluded forest. It will become the place of burial for the University. Here will the dust of the young men, who may be cut off before their academic course is run, be laid by their class-mates. Here will be deposited those who may die in the offices of instruction and government. Nor is it impossible, that the several class-associations, which form a beautiful feature of our college life, may each appropriate to themselves a lot, where such of their brethren as may desire it, may be brought back to be deposited in the soil of the spot where they passed their early years.

The establishment contemplated will afford the means of paying a tribute of respect, by a monumental erection, to the names and memory of great and good men, whenever or wherever they have died. Its summit may be consecrated to Washington, by a cenotaph inscribed with his name. Public sentiment will often delight in these tributes of respect, and the place may gradually become the honorary mausoleum for the distinguished sons of Massachusetts.

This design, though but recently made public, has been long in contemplation, and, as is believed, has been favored with unusual approbation. It has drawn forth much unsolicited and earnest concurrence. It has touched a chord of sympathy which vibrates in every heart. Let us take an affectionate and pious care of our dead; let us turn to some good account, in softening and humanizing the public feeling, that sentiment of tenderness toward the departed, which is natural and ineradicable in man. Let us employ some of the superfluous wealth, now often expended in luxury worse than useless, in rendering the

place where our beloved friends repose, decent,
attractive, and grateful at once to the eye and the
heart.

AN ADDRESS DELIVERED ON THE DEDICATION OF
THE CEMETERY AT MOUNT AUBURN, SEPTEM-
BER 24TH, 1831. BY JOSEPH STORY.

MY FRIENDS, —

THE occasion which brings us together, has
much in it calculated to awaken our sensibilities,
and cast a solemnity over our thoughts.

We are met to consecrate these grounds exclusively to the service and repose of the dead.

The duty is not new; for it has been performed
for countless millions. The scenery is not new;
for the hill and the valley, the still, silent dell, and
the deep forest, have often been devoted to the
same pious purpose. But that, which must always
give it a peculiar interest, is, that it can rarely
occur except at distant intervals; and, whenever
it does, it must address itself to feelings intelligible
to all nations, and common to all hearts.

The patriarchal language of four thousand years

ago is precisely that, to which we would now give utterance. We are "strangers and sojourners" here. We have need of "a possession of a burying-place, that we may bury our dead out of our sight." Let us have "the field, and the cave which is therein; and all the trees, that are in the field, and that are in the borders round about;" and let them "be made sure for a possession of a burying-place."

It is the duty of the living thus to provide for the dead. It is not a mere office of pious regard for others; but it comes home to our own bosoms, as those who are soon to enter upon the common inheritance.

If there are any feelings of our nature, not bounded by earth, and yet stopping short of the skies, which are more strong and more universal than all others, they will be found in our solicitude as to the time and place and manner of our death; in the desire to die in the arms of our friends; to have the last sad offices to our remains performed by their affection; to repose in the land of our nativity; to be gathered to the sepulchres of our fathers. It is almost impossible for us to feel, nay, even to feign, indifference on such a subject.

Poetry has told us this truth in lines of trans-

cendent beauty and force, which find a response
in every breast : —

> " For who, to dumb Forgetfulness a prey,
>> This pleasing, anxious being e'er resigned,
> Left the warm precincts of the cheerful day,
>> Nor cast one longing, lingering look behind ?
>
> On some fond breast the parting soul relies;
>> Some pious drops the closing eye requires;
> E'en from the tomb the voice of Nature cries;
>> E'en in our ashes live their wonted fires."

It is in vain, that Philosophy has informed us,
that the whole earth is but a point in the eyes of
its Creator, — nay, of his own creation ; that,
wherever we are, — abroad or at home, — on the
restless ocean, or the solid land, — we are still
under the protection of his providence, and safe,
as it were, in the hollow of his hand. It is in
vain that Religion has instructed us, that we are
but dust, and to dust we shall return, — that
whether our remains are scattered to the corners
of the earth, or gathered in sacred urns, there is a
sure and certain hope of a resurrection of the body
and a life everlasting. These truths, sublime and
glorious as they are, leave untouched the feelings,
of which I have spoken, or, rather, they impart
to them a more enduring reality. Dust as we are,

10

the frail tenements, which enclose our spirits but for a season, are dear, are inexpressibly dear to us. We derive solace, nay, pleasure from the reflection, that when the hour of separation comes, these earthly remains will still retain the tender regard of those whom we leave behind; — that the spot, where they shall lie, will be remembered with a fond and soothing reverence; — that our children will visit it in the midst of their sorrows; and our kindred in remote generations feel that a local inspiration hovers round it.

Let him speak, who has been on a pilgrimage of health to a foreign land. Let him speak, who has watched at the couch of a dying friend, far from his chosen home. Let him speak, who has committed to the bosom of the deep, with a sudden, startling plunge, the narrow shroud of some relative or companion. Let such speak, and they will tell you, that there is nothing which wrings the heart of the dying, — ay, and of the surviving, — with sharper agony, than the thought, that they are to sleep their last sleep in the land of strangers, or in the unseen depths of the ocean.

" Bury me not, I pray thee," said the patriarch Jacob, " bury me not in Egypt : but I will lie with my fathers. And thou shalt carry me out

of Egypt; and bury me in their burying place."
—"There they buried Abraham and Sarah his
wife; there they buried Isaac and Rebecca his
wife; and there I buried Leah."

Such are the natural expressions of human feeling, as they fall from the lips of the dying. Such
are the reminiscences, that forever crowd on the
confines of the passes to the grave. We seek
again to have our home there with our friends,
and to be blest by a communion with them. It
is a matter of instinct, not of reasoning. It is a
spiritual impulse, which supersedes belief, and
disdains question.

But it is not chiefly in regard to the feelings
belonging to our own mortality, however sacred
and natural, that we should contemplate the establishment of repositories of this sort. There are
higher moral purposes, and more affecting considerations, which belong to the subject. We
should accustom ourselves to view them rather
as means, than as ends; rather as influences to
govern human conduct, and to moderate human
suffering, than as cares incident to a selfish foresight.

It is to the living mourner — to the parent,
weeping over his dear dead child — to the hus-

band, dwelling in his own solitary desolation —
to the widow, whose heart is broken by untimely
sorrow — to the friend, who misses at every turn
the presence of some kindred spirit : — it is to
these, that the repositories of the dead bring home
thoughts full of admonition, of instruction, and,
slowly but surely, of consolation also. They ad-
monish us, by their very silence, of our own frail
and transitory being. They instruct us in the
true value of life, and in its noble purposes, its
duties, and its destination. They spread around
us, in the reminiscences of the past, sources of
pleasing, though melancholy reflection.

We dwell with pious fondness on the characters
and virtues of the departed ; and, as time inter-
poses its growing distances between us and them,
we gather up, with more solicitude, the broken
fragments of memory, and weave, as it were, into
our very hearts, the threads of their history. As
we sit down by their graves, we seem to hear the
tones of their affection, whispering in our ears.
We listen to the voice of their wisdom, speaking
in the depths of our souls. We shed our tears ;
but they are no longer the burning tears of agony.
They relieve our drooping spirits, and come no
longer over us with a deathly faintness. We

return to the world, and we feel ourselves purer, and better, and wiser, from this communion with the dead.

I have spoken but of feelings and associations common to all ages, and all generations of men — to the rude and the polished — to the barbarian and the civilized — to the bond and the free — to the inhabitant of the dreary forests of the north, and the sultry regions of the south — to the worshipper of the sun, and the worshipper of idols — to the Heathen, dwelling in the darkness of his cold mythology, and to the Christian, rejoicing in the light of the true God. Everywhere we trace them in the characteristic remains of the most distant ages and nations, and as far back as human history carries its traditionary outlines. They are found in the barrows, and cairns, and mounds of olden times, reared by the uninstructed affection of savage tribes; and, everywhere, the spots seem to have been selected with the same tender regard to the living and the dead ; that the magnificence of nature might administer comfort to human sorrow, and incite human sympathy.

The aboriginal Germans buried their dead in groves consecrated by their priests. The Egyptians gratified their pride and soothed their grief,

by interring them in their Elysian fields, or em-
balming them in their vast catacombs, or enclosing
them in their stupendous pyramids, the wonder of
all succeeding ages.   The Hebrews watched with
religious care over their places of burial.   They
selected, for this purpose, ornamented gardens and
deep forests, and fertile valleys, and lofty mountains ; and they still designate them with a sad
emphasis, as the "House of the Living."   The
ancient Asiatics lined the approaches to their cities
with sculptured sarcophagi, and mausoleums, and
other ornaments, embowered in shrubbery, traces of
which may be seen among their magnificent ruins.
The Greeks exhausted the resources of their exquisite art in adorning the habitations of the
dead.   They discouraged interments within the
limits of their cities ; and consigned their relics
to shady groves, in the neighborhood of murmur-
ing streams and mossy fountains, close by the
favorite resorts of those who were engaged in the
study of philosophy and nature, and called them,
with the elegant expressiveness of their own beautiful language, CEMETERIES,* or "Places of
Repose."   The Romans, faithful to the example

* Χοιμητηρια — literally, places of sleep

of Greece, erected the monuments to the dead in
the suburbs of the eternal city, (as they proudly
denominated it,) on the sides of their spacious
roads, in the midst of trees and ornamental walks,
and ever-varying flowers. The Appian Way was
crowded with columns, and obelisks, and cenotaphs
to the memory of her heroes and sages ; and, at
every turn, the short but touching inscription met
the eye, — Siste Viator, — Pause Traveller, —
inviting at once to sympathy and thoughtfulness.
Even the humblest Roman could read on the
humblest gravestone the kind offering — " May
the earth lie lightly on these remains ! "* And
the Moslem Successors of the emperors, indifferent
as they may be to the ordinary exhibitions of the
fine arts, place their burying-grounds in rural
retreats, and embellish them with studious taste
as a religious duty. The cypress is planted at
the head and foot of every grave, and waves with
a mournful solemnity over it. These devoted
grounds possess an inviolable sanctity. The rav-
ages of war never reach them ; and victory and
defeat equally respect the limits of their domain.
So that it has been remarked, with equal truth

* " Sit tibi terra levis."

and beauty, that while the cities of the living are subject to all the desolations and vicissitudes incident to human affairs, the cities of the dead enjoy an undisturbed repose, without even the shadow of change.

But I will not dwell upon facts of this nature. They demonstrate, however, the truth, of which I have spoken. They do more; they furnish reflections suitable for our own thoughts on the present occasion.

If this tender regard for the dead be so absolutely universal, and so deeply founded in human affection, why is it not made to exert a more profound influence on our lives? Why do we not enlist it with more persuasive energy in the cause of human improvement? Why do we not enlarge it as a source of religious consolation? Why do we not make it a more efficient instrument to elevate Ambition, to stimulate Genius, and to dignify Learning? Why do we not connect it indissolubly with associations, which charm us in Nature and engross us in Art? Why do we not dispel from it that unlovely gloom, from which our hearts turn as from a darkness that ensnares, and a horror that appals our thoughts?

To many, nay, to most of the heathen, the

burying-place was the end of all things. They indulged no hope, at least, no solid hope, of any future intercourse or re-union with their friends. The farewell at the grave was a long, and an everlasting farewell. At the moment, when they breathed it, it brought to their hearts a startling sense of their own wretchedness. Yet, when the first tumults of anguish were passed, they visited the spot, and strewed flowers, and garlands, and crowns around it, to assuage their grief, and nourish their piety. They delighted to make it the abode of the varying beauties of Nature; to give it attractions, which should invite the busy and the thoughtful; and yet, at the same time, afford ample scope for the secret indulgence of sorrow.

Why should not Christians imitate such examples? They have far nobler motives to cultivate moral sentiments and sensibilities; to make cheerful the pathways to the grave; to combine with deep meditations on human mortality the sublime consolations of religion. We know, indeed, as they did of old, that "man goeth to his long home, and the mourners go about the streets." But that home is not an everlasting home; and the mourners may not weep as those who are without hope. What is the grave to Us, but a

thin barrier dividing Time from Eternity, and
Earth from Heaven? What is it but "the appointed place of rendezvous, where all the travellers on life's journey meet" for a single night of
repose ?

> " 'Tis but a night — a long and moonless night,
>   We make the Grave our Bed, and then are gone."

Know we not

> —— " The time draws on
>   When not a single spot of burial earth,
>   Whether on land, or in the spacious sea,
>   But must give up its long committed dust
>   Inviolate ? " —

Why then should we darken with systematic
caution all the avenues to these repositories?
Why should we deposit the remains of our friends
in loathsome vaults, or beneath the gloomy crypts
and cells of our churches, where the human foot
is never heard, save when the sickly taper lights
some new guest to his appointed apartment, and
" lets fall a supernumerary horror " on the passing
procession? Why should we measure out a narrow portion of earth for our graveyards in the
midst of our cities, and heap the dead upon each
other with a cold, calculating parsimony, disturbing their ashes, and wounding the sensibilities of

the living? Why should we expose our burying-grounds to the broad glare of day, to the unfeeling gaze of the idler, to the noisy press of business, to the discordant shouts of merriment, or to the baleful visitations of the dissolute? Why should we bar up their approaches against real mourners, whose delicacy would shrink from observation, but whose tenderness would be soothed by secret visits to the grave, and holding converse there with their departed joys? Why all this unnatural restraint upon our sympathies and sorrows, which confines the visit to the grave to the only time, in which it must be utterly useless — when the heart is bleeding with fresh anguish, and is too weak to feel, and too desolate to desire consolation?

It is painful to reflect, that the Cemeteries in our cities, crowded on all sides by the overhanging habitations of the living, are walled in only to preserve them from violation. And that in our country towns they are left in a sad, neglected state, exposed to every sort of intrusion, with scarcely a tree to shelter their barrenness, or a shrub to spread a grateful shade over the new-made hillock.

These things were not always so among Christians. They are not worthy of us. They are not worthy of Christianity in our day. There is much in these things, that casts a just reproach upon us in the past. There is much that demands for the future a more spiritual discharge of our duties.

Our Cemeteries rightly selected, and properly arranged, may be made subservient to some of the highest purposes of religion and human duty. They may preach lessons, to which none may refuse to listen, and which all, that live, must hear. Truths may be there felt and taught in the silence of our own meditations, more persuasive, and more enduring, than ever flowed from human lips. The grave hath a voice of eloquence, nay, of superhuman eloquence, which speaks at once to the thoughtlessness of the rash, and the devotion of the good; which addresses all times, and all ages, and all sexes; which tells of wisdom to the wise, and of comfort to the afflicted; which warns us of our follies and our dangers; which whispers to us in accents of peace, and alarms us in tones of terror; which steals with a healing balm into the stricken heart, and lifts up and supports the broken spirit; which awakens a new enthusiasm for virtue, and disciplines us for its severer trials and duties ; which calls up the images of the illustrious dead, with an animating presence for our example and glory ; and which demands of us, as men, as patriots, as Christians, as immortals, that the powers given by God should be devoted to his service, and the minds created by his love, should return to him with larger capacities for virtuous enjoyment, and with more spiritual and intellectual brightness.

It should not be for the poor purpose of gratifying our vanity or pride, that we should erect columns, and obelisks, and monuments, to the dead ; but that we may read thereon much of our own destiny and duty. We know, that man is the creature of associations and excitements. Experience may instruct, but habit, and appetite, and passion, and imagination, will exercise a strong dominion over him. These are the Fates, which weave the thread of his character, and unravel the mysteries of his conduct. The truth, which strikes home, must not only have the approbation of his reason, but it must be embodied in a visible, tangible, practical form. It must be felt, as well as seen. It must warm, as well as convince.

It was a saying of Themistocles, that the trophies of Miltiades would not suffer him to sleep.

The feeling, thus expressed, has a deep foundation
in the human mind ; and, as it is well or ill directed, it will cover us with shame, or exalt us
to glory.   The deeds of the great attract but a
cold and listless admiration, when they pass in
historical order before us like moving shadows.
It is the trophy and the monument, which invest
them with a substance of local reality.   Who,
that has stood by the tomb of Washington on the
quiet Potomac, has not felt his heart more pure,
his wishes more aspiring, his gratitude more warm,
and his love of country touched by a holier flame?
Who, that should see erected in shades, like
these, even a cenotaph to the memory of a man,
like Buckminster, that prodigy of early genius,
would not feel, that there is an excellence over
which death hath no power, but which lives on
through all time, still freshening with the lapse
of ages.

But passing from those, who by their talents
and virtues have shed lustre on the annals of mankind, to cases of mere private bereavement, who,
that should deposit in shades, like these, the
remains of a beloved friend, would not feel a
secret pleasure in the thought, that the simple
inscription to his worth would receive the passing

tribute of a sigh from thousands of kindred hearts?
That the stranger and the traveller would linger
on the spot with a feeling of reverence? That
they, the very mourners themselves, when they
should revisit it, would find there the verdant sod,
and the fragrant flower, and the breezy shade?
That they might there, unseen, except of God,
offer up their prayers, or indulge the luxury of
grief? That they might there realize, in its full
force, the affecting beatitude of the Scriptures:
" Blessed are they that mourn, for they shall be
comforted?"

Surely, surely, we have not done all our duty,
if there yet remains a single incentive to human
virtue, without its due play in the action of life,
or a single stream of happiness, which has not been
made to flow in upon the waters of affliction.

Considerations, like those, which have been suggested, have for a long time turned the thoughts
of many distinguished citizens to the importance of
some more appropriate places of sepulture. There
is a growing sense in the community of the inconveniences, and painful associations, not to speak
of the unhealthiness of interments, beneath our
churches. The tide, which is flowing with such
a steady and widening current into the narrow

peninsula of our Metropolis, not only forbids the enlargement of the common limits, but admonishes us of the increasing dangers to the ashes of the dead from its disturbing movements. Already in other cities, the churchyards are closing against the admission of new incumbents, and begin to exhibit the sad spectacle of promiscuous ruins and intermingled graves.

We are, therefore, but anticipating at the present moment, the desires, nay, the necessities of the next generation. We are but exercising a decent anxiety to secure an inviolable home for ourselves and our posterity. We are but inviting our children and their descendants, to what the Moravian Brothers have, with such exquisite propriety, designated as " the Field of Peace."

A rural Cemetery seems to combine in itself all the advantages, which can be proposed to gratify human feelings, or tranquillize human fears ; to secure the best religious influences, and to cherish all those associations which cast a cheerful light over the darkness of the grave.

And what spot can be more appropriate than this, for such a purpose? Nature seems to point it out with significant energy, as the favorite retirement for the dead. There are around us all

the varied features of her beauty and grandeur —
'the forest-crowned height; the abrupt acclivity;
the sheltered valley; the deep glen; the grassy
glade; and the silent grove.   Here are the lofty
oak, the beech, that "wreaths its old fantastic
roots so high," the rustling pine, and the drooping
willow; — the tree, that sheds its pale leaves with
every autumn, a fit emblem of our own transitory
bloom; and the evergreen, with its perennial
shoots, instructing us, that "the wintry blast of
death kills not the buds of virtue."   Here is the
thick shrubbery to protect and conceal the new-
made grave; and there is the wild-flower creeping
along the narrow path, and planting its seeds in
the upturned earth.   All around us there breathes
a solemn calm, as if we were in the bosom of a
wilderness, broken only by the breeze as it mur-
murs through the tops of the forest, or by the notes
of the warbler pouring forth his matin or his evening song.

Ascend but a few steps, and what a change of
scenery to surprise and delight us.   We seem, as
it were in an instant, to pass from the confines of
death, to the bright and balmy regions of life.
Below us flows the winding Charles with its rip-
pling current, like the stream of time hastening

11

to the ocean of eternity. In the distance, the City, — at once the object of our admiration and our love, — rears its proud eminences, its glittering spires, its lofty towers, its graceful mansions, its curling smoke, its crowded haunts of business and pleasure, which speak to the eye, and yet leave a noiseless loneliness on the ear. Again we turn, and the walls of our venerable University rise before us, with many a recollection of happy days passed there in the interchange of study and friendship, and many a grateful thought of the affluence of its learning, which has adorned and nourished the literature of our country. Again we turn, and the cultivated farm, the neat cottage, the village church, the sparkling lake, the rich valley, and the distant hills, are before us through opening vistas ; and we breathe amidst the fresh and varied labors of man.

There is, therefore, within our reach, every variety of natural and artificial scenery, which is fitted to awaken emotions of the highest and most affecting character. We stand, as it were, upon the borders of two worlds ; and as the mood of our minds may be, we may gather lessons of profound wisdom by contrasting the one with the other, or indulge in the dreams of hope and ambition, or solace our hearts by melancholy meditations.

Who is there, that in the contemplation of such a scene, is not ready to exclaim with the enthusiasm of the Poet,

" Mine be the breezy hill, that skirts the down,
    Where a green, grassy turf is all I crave,
  With here and there a violet bestrown,
    Fast by a brook, or fountain's murmuring wave,
    And many an evening's sun shine sweetly on my grave ? "

And we are met here to consecrate this spot, by these solemn ceremonies, to such a purpose. The Legislature of this Commonwealth, with a parental foresight, has clothed the Horticultural Society with authority (if I may use its own language) to make a perpetual dedication of it, as a Rural Cemetery or Burying-Ground, and to plant and embellish it with shrubbery, and flowers, and trees, and walks, and other rural ornaments. And I stand here by the order and in behalf of this Society, to declare that, by these services, it is to be deemed henceforth and forever so dedicated. Mount Auburn, in the noblest sense, belongs no longer to the living, but to the dead. It is a sacred, it is an eternal trust. It is consecrated ground. May it remain forever inviolate !

What a multitude of thoughts crowd upon the

mind in the contemplation of such a scene. How much of the future, even in its far distant reaches, rises before us with all its persuasive realities. Take but one little narrow space of time, and how affecting are its associations! Within the flight of one half century, how many of the great, the good, and the wise, will be gathered here! How many in the loveliness of infancy, the beauty of youth, the vigor of manhood, and the maturity of age, will lie down here, and dwell in the bosom of their mother earth! The rich and the poor, the gay and the wretched, the favorites of thousands, and the forsaken of the world, the stranger in his solitary grave, and the patriarch surrounded by the kindred of a long lineage! How many will here bury their brightest hopes, or blasted expectations! How many bitter tears will here be shed! How many agonizing sighs will here be heaved! How many trembling feet will cross the pathways, and returning, leave behind them the dearest objects of their reverence or their love!

And if this were all, sad indeed, and funereal would be our thoughts; gloomy, indeed, would be these shades, and desolate these prospects.

But — thanks be to God — the evils, which he permits, have their attendant mercies, and are blessings in disguise. The bruised reed will not be laid utterly prostrate. The wounded heart will not always bleed. The voice of consolation will spring up in the midst of the silence of these regions of death. The mourner will revisit these shades with a secret, though melancholy pleasure. The hand of friendship will delight to cherish the flowers, and the shrubs, that fringe the lowly grave, or the sculptured monument. The earliest beams of the morning will play upon these summits with a refreshing cheerfulness; and the lingering tints of evening hover on them with a tranquillizing glow. Spring will invite thither the footsteps of the young by its opening foliage; and Autumn detain the contemplative by its latest bloom. The votary of learning and science will here learn to elevate his genius by the holiest of studies. The devout will here offer up the silent tribute of pity, or the prayer of gratitude. The rivalries of the world will here drop from the heart; the spirit of forgiveness will gather new impulses; the selfishness of avarice will be checked; the restlessness of ambition will be rebuked; vanity will let fall its plumes; and pride, as it sees " what shadows we are, and what shadows we pursue," will acknowledge the value of virtue as far, immeasurably far, beyond that of fame.

But that, which will be ever present, pervading these shades, like the noon-day sun, and shedding cheerfulness around, is the consciousness, the irrepressible consciousness, amidst all these lessons of human mortality, of the higher truth, that we are beings, not of time but of eternity — " That this corruptible must put on incorruption, and this mortal must put on immortality." That this is but the threshold and starting point of an existence, compared with whose duration the ocean is but as a drop, nay, the whole creation an evanescent quantity.

Let us banish, then, the thought, that this is to be the abode of a gloom, which will haunt the imagination by its terrors, or chill the heart by its solitude. Let us cultivate feelings and sentiments more worthy of ourselves, and more worthy of Christianity. Here let us erect the memorials of our love, and our gratitude, and our glory. Here let the brave repose, who have died in the cause of their country. Here let the statesman rest, who has achieved the victories of peace, not less renowned than war. Here let genius find a home, that has sung immortal strains, or has instructed

with still diviner eloquence. Here let learning
and science, the votaries of inventive art, and the
teacher of the philosophy of nature come. Here
let youth and beauty, blighted by premature decay,
drop, like tender blossoms, into the virgin earth;
and here let age retire, ripened for the harvest.
Above all, here let the benefactors of mankind,
the good, the merciful, the meek, the pure in
heart, be congregated; for to them belongs an
undying praise. And let us take comfort, nay,
let us rejoice, that in future ages, long after we are
gathered to the generations of other days, thousands of kindling hearts will here repeat the
sublime declaration, " Blessed are the dead, that
die in the Lord, for they rest from their labors;
and their works do follow them."

A REPORT ON THE GARDEN AND CEMETERY.

By H. A. S. Dearborn.

At the Annual Meeting of the Horticultural Society, September 30th, 1831, the Committee on laying out the grounds and forming the plan of the Experimental Garden and Cemetery at Mount Auburn, made the following

REPORT,

" That measures were promptly taken for accomplishing those objects, and although considerable progress has been made, it will require further time to complete the work.

Alexander Wadsworth, Esq., a skilful civil engineer, was employed to make an accurate topographical survey, and to locate the numerous avenues, which it was found necessary to establish through the extensive and beautifully diversified grounds of the Cemetery and Garden, both for convenience and embellishment. The map has been so far perfected, that it is submitted for inspection, and to exhibit the general outlines of the projected improvements; but considerable labor is yet required in clearing out the principal carriage avenues and foot paths, before the sites of the public and private cemetery squares can be definitely established, and designated on the plan.

Models and drawings of the Egyptian Gateways, and of a Gothic tower, and a Grecian
tower, one of which is proposed to be erected on
the highest hill, have been made, and are offered
for examination.

It has been ascertained, that the most lofty
eminence is one hundred and twenty-five feet
above Charles River, which gracefully sweeps
round its gently sloping base ; and when crowned
by the proposed tower, will become a most interesting place of resort, as commanding an extensive
panoramic view of that richly variegated region of
magnificent scenery, embraced within the far distant heights which encircle the metropolis, and
the waves of the ocean ; while it will present a
prominent and imposing feature in the landscape,
of which it becomes the centre.

At some future period, when the munificence
of the citizens shall be commensurate with their
debt of patriotic gratitude, this structure may perhaps give place for a stupendous monument to
the most illustrious benefactor of his country ; —
there will be reared the cenotaph of Washington,
in massive blocks of granite or ever-during marble. Should the funds hereafter justify it, a
Doric Temple, to be used as a chapel, for the

performance of funeral rites, and lodges for the gardener and superintendent of the Cemetery, are contemplated, and designs are in progress for each.

As the season for rural labor is far advanced, it is not considered expedient to commence the construction of the avenues before the next spring; but they can be divested of the underwood, and the whole of the grounds so far cleared up, as to give them the appearance of a park, during the present autumn. It is expected that the lots may be assigned within twenty days,

The Committee has been cheered, in the discharge of its duties, by the deep interest which has been manifested for the success of an undertaking, so important to the prosperity of the Horticultural Society, and so honorable to the country. Such is the exalted estimation in which it is held by the public, so universal is the approbation, so intense the interest, that beside the constant requests for permission to become subscribers, by the more affluent, numerous applications have been made for Cemetery lots, by farmers, mechanics, and dealers in building materials, on condition, that they may be paid for in labor, or such articles as shall be required in the prosecution of the proposed improvements. Within a few days offers have been made to a considerable amount; and as it was the intention and is the anxious desire of the Society, that every citizen should have an opportunity of participating in the advantages of the establishment, the committee has availed itself of the services thus tendered, in executing much of the work which has been performed; and there is not a doubt, that a very considerable portion of the expense in constructing roads, fences, gateways, and the various other edifices, may be defrayed, by a compensation in Cemetery lots. This will not only be a great accommodation to numerous individuals, who are desirous to become subscribers, but be highly advantageous to the Society. It is therefore recommended, that the Committee be authorized to prosecute such improvements as may be deemed necessary, on these reciprocally beneficial terms.

With the view of fully meeting the expectations and exigencies of the community, it is considered advisable that sites for single graves should be designated, in various parts of the Cemetery, embracing all the diversified localities, to afford an opportunity for individuals, who have no families, and the friends of such strangers as may be wept and honored far distant from their native land, to procure eligible places of sepulture, on reasonable terms.

As the tract which has been solemnly consecrated, by religious ceremonies, as a burial place forever, is so abundantly covered with forest trees, many of which are more than sixty years old, it only requires the avenues to be formed, the borders, for some ten feet in width, planted with shrubs, bulbous and perennial flowers, the underwood cleared out, the fences, gateways, and appropriate edifices erected, to put the grounds in a sufficiently complete state for the uses designed, and to render them at once beautiful and interesting. All this can be done within two years, at a comparatively small expense, and a result produced which could not have been realized for forty years, if it had been necessary to commence the establishment by planting out forest trees. There are numerous majestic oaks, pines, beeches, and walnuts, which have braved the storms of a century. Towering aloft amidst the general verdure, and extending their huge branches far and wide, they appear as the venerable monarchs of the grove, but still exhibit the vigor of their luxuriant progeny, which, in umbrageous contiguity, cover each hill and plain, and sloping vale, and form many an

> ———— " alley green,
> Dingle, or bushy dell, in this wild wood,
> And many a bosky bourn, from side to side "

The Garden also can be very considerably advanced, within the same short period which will suffice for developing the improvements of the Cemetery. The nurseries may be established, the departments for culinary vegetables, fruit, and ornamental trees, shrubs and flowers, laid out and planted, a green-house built, hot-beds formed, the small ponds and morasses converted into picturesque sheets of water, and their margins diversified by clumps and belts of our most splendid native flowering trees and shrubs, requiring a soil thus constituted for their successful cultivation, while their surface may be spangled with the brilliant blossoms of the Nymphæa, and the other beautiful tribes of aquatic plants. The excavations for deepening and enlarging the ponds and morasses will afford inexhaustible sources of manure, of invaluable consequence to the Garden, as well as for those portions of the Cemetery which will be embellished by cultivated plants.

From these favorable circumstances and the

generous zeal which has been evinced for the energetic prosecution of the labors, which are required to perfect the details of the whole extensive plan, there no longer remains the least doubt, that in the summer of 1834, Mount Auburn will rival the most celebrated rural burial grounds of Europe, and present a garden in such a state of forwardness, as will be highly gratifying to the Society and the public. The work has been commenced on an ever-during foundation, has the approbation and patronage of an enterprising, intelligent, and prosperous community, and cannot fail of progressing in a manner that must give universal satisfaction. There has Horticulture established her temple, — there will all denominations of Christians surrender up their prejudices, . — there will repose the ashes of the humble and exalted, in the silent and sacred Garden of the Dead, until summoned to those of eternal life, in realms beyond the skies.

Respectfully submitted by

H. A. S. DEARBORN,
For the Committee."

A DISCOURSE ON THE BURIAL OF THE DEAD.
By Jacob Bigelow.

While the subject of Mount Auburn was of recent agitation,
the following Address was delivered at the hall of the Masonic
Temple, in 1831, before the Boston Society for the Promotion of
Useful Knowledge · —

" The manner in which we dispose of the remains of our deceased friends, is a subject which,
within the last few years, has occupied a greater
share than formerly of the public attention in our
own vicinity.   It involves not only considerations
which belong to the general convenience, but
includes also the gratification of individual taste,
and the consolation of private sorrow.   Although,
in a strictly philosophical view, this subject possesses but little importance, except in relation to
the convenience of survivors ; yet so closely are
our sympathies enlisted with it, so inseparably do
we connect the feelings of the living with the condition of the dead, that it is in vain that we
attempt to divest ourselves of its influence.   It is
incumbent on us therefore to analyze, as far as

we may be able, the principles which belong to a correct view of this subject; since it is only by understanding these, that we may expect both reason.and feeling to be satisfied.

The progress of all organized beings is towards decay. The complicated textures which the living body elaborates within itself, begin to fall asunder almost as soon as life has ceased. The materials of which animals and vegetables are composed, have natural laws and irresistible affinities which are suspended during the period of life, but which must be obeyed the moment that life is extinct. These continue to operate, until the exquisite fabric is reduced to a condition, in no wise different from that of the soil on which it has once trodden. In certain cases art may modify, and accident may retard, the approaches of disorganization, but the exceptions thus produced are too few and imperfect, to invalidate the certainty of the general law.

If we take a comprehensive survey of the progress and mutations of animal and vegetable life, we shall perceive that this necessity of individual destruction is the basis of general safety. The elements which have once moved and circulated in living frames do not become extinct nor useless after death : they offer themselves as the materials from which other living frames are to constructed. What has once possessed life is most assimilated to the living character, and most ready to partake of life again. The plant which springs from the earth, after attaining its growth and perpetuating its species, falls to the ground, undergoes decomposition, and contributes its remains to the nourishment of plants around it. The myriads of animals which range the woods, or inhabit the air, at length die upon the surface of the earth, and, if not devoured by other animals, prepare for vegetation the place which receives their remains. Were it not for this law of nature, the soil would be soon exhausted, the earth's surface would become a barren waste, and the whole race of organized beings, for want of sustenance, would become extinct.

Man alone, the master of the creation, does not willingly stoop to become a participator in the routine of nature. In every age he has manifested a disposition to exempt himself, and to rescue his fellow, from the common fate of living beings. Although he is prodigal of the lives of other classes, and sometimes sacrifices a hundred inferior bodies, to procure himself a single repast,

12

yet he regards with scrupulous anxiety the destination of his own remains ; and much labor and treasure are devoted by him to ward off, for a season, t' e inevitable courses of nature. Under the apprehension of posthumous degradation, human bodies have been embalmed, their concentrated dust has been inclosed in golden urns, monumental fortresses have been piled over their decaying bones ; — with what success, and with what use, it may not be amiss to consider.

I have selected a few instances, in which measures have been taken to protect the human frame from decay, which will be seen to have been in some cases partially successful, in others not so. They will serve as preliminaries to the general considerations which are connected with the subject. .

One of the most interesting accounts of the preservation of a body, the identity of which was undoubted, is that of the disinterment of King Edward I. of England. The readers of English History will recollect that this monarch gave, as a dying charge to his son, that his heart should be sent to the Holy Land, but that his body should be carried in the van of the army till Scotland was reduced to obedience.

He died in July, 1307, and notwithstanding his injunctions, was buried in Westminster Abbey in October of the same year. It is recorded that he was embalmed, and orders for renewing the cere-cloth about his body were issued in the reigns of Edward III. and Henry IV. The tomb of this monarch was opened, and his body examined in January, 1774, under the direction of Sir Joseph Ayloffe, after it had been buried four hundred and sixty-seven years. The following account is extracted from a contemporaneous volume of the Gentleman's Magazine : —

'Some gentlemen of the Society of Antiquaries, being desirous to see how far the actual state of Edward First's body answered to the methods taken to preserve it, obtained leave to open the large stone sarcophagus, in which it is known to have been deposited, on the north side of Edward the Confessor's chapel. This was accordingly done on the morning of January 2, 1774, when in a coffin of yellow stone, they found the royal body in perfect preservation, inclosed in two wrappers ; one of them was of gold tissue, strongly waxed, and fresh, the other and outermost considerably decayed. The corpse was habited in a rich mantle of purple, paned with white, and adorned with ornaments of gilt metal, studded with red and blue stones and pearls. Two similar ornaments lay on the hands. The mantle was fastened on the right shoulder by a magnificent *fibula* of the same metal, with the same stones and pearls. His face had over it a silken covering, so fine, and so closely fitted to it, as to preserve the features entire. Round his temples was a gilt coronet of fleurs de lys. In his hands, which were also entire, were two sceptres of gilt metal; that in the right surmounted by a cross fleure, that in the left by three clusters of oak leaves, and a dove on a globe; this sceptre was about five feet long. The feet were enveloped in the mantle and other coverings, but sound, and the toes distinct. The whole length of the corpse was five feet two inches.'

This last statement, it will be observed, is the only point in which the narrative appears to disagree with history. We are generally given to understand that Edward I. was a tall man; and that he was designated in his own time by the name of Long-shanks. Baker, in his Chronicle of the Kings of England, says of him that he was tall of stature, exceeding most other men by a head and shoulders. I have not been able to find Sir Joseph Ayloffe's account of the examination, and know of no other mode of reconciling the discrepancy, but by supposing a typographical error of a figure in the account which has been quoted.

Edward I. died at Burgh-upon-Sands, in Cumberland, on his way to Scotland, July 7, 1307, in the sixty-eighth year of his age.

Another instance of partial preservation, is that of the body of King Charles I., who was beheaded by his subjects in 1649. The remains of this unfortunate monarch are known to have been carried to Windsor, and there interred by his friends without pomp, in a hasty and private manner. It is stated in Clarendon's History of the Rebellion, that when his son, Charles II., was desirous to remove and re-inter his corpse at Westminster Abbey, it could not by any search be found In constructing a mausoleum at Windsor in 1813, under the direction of George IV., then Prince Regent, an accident led to the discovery of this royal body. The workmen, in forming a subterraneous passage under the choir of St. George's Chapel, accidentally made an

aperture in the wall of the vault of King Henry
VIII. On looking through this opening it was
found to contain three coffins, instead of two, as
had been supposed. Two of these were ascertained to be the coffins of Henry VIII., and one
of his queens, Jane Seymour. The other was
formally examined, after permission obtained, by
Sir Henry Halford, in presence of several members of the royal family, and other persons of
distinction. The account since published by Sir
Henry, corroborates the one which had been given
by Mr. Herbert, a groom of King Charles's bed-
chamber, and is published in Wood's Athenæ
Oxonienses.

'On removing the pall,' says the account, 'a
plain leaden coffin presented itself to view, with
no appearance of ever having been inclosed in
wood, and bearing an inscription, "King Charles,
1648," in large, legible characters, on a scroll of
lead encircling it. A square opening was then
made in the upper part of the lid, of such dimensions as to admit a clear insight into its contents.
These were, an internal wooden coffin, very much
decayed, and the body carefully wrapped up in
cere-cloth, into the folds of which a quantity of

unctuous matter, mixed with resin, as it seemed, had been melted, so as to exclude, as effectually as possible, the external air. The coffin was completely full, and, from the tenacity of the cere-cloth, great difficulty was experienced in detaching it successfully from the parts which it enveloped. Wherever the unctuous matter had insinuated itself, the separation of the cere-cloth was easy; and where it came off, a correct impression of the features to which it had been applied, was observed. At length the whole face was disengaged from its covering. The complexion of the skin of it was dark and discolored. The forehead and temples had lost little or nothing of their muscular substance; the cartilage of the nose was gone; but the left eye, in the first moment of exposure, was open and full, though it vanished almost immediately; and the pointed beard, so characteristic of the period of the reign of King Charles, was perfect. The shape of the face was a long oval; many of the teeth remained; and the left ear, in consequence of the interposition of the unctuous matter between it and the cere-cloth, was found entire.

'It was difficult, at this moment, to withhold a declaration, that, notwithstanding its disfigurement, the countenance did bear a strong resemblance to the coins, the busts, and especially to the picture of King Charles the First, by Vandyke, by which it had been made familiar to us. It is true, that the minds of the spectators of this interesting sight were well prepared to receive this impression; but it is also certain that such a facility of belief had been occasioned by the simplicity and truth of Mr. Herbert's Narrative, every part of which had been confirmed by the investigation, so far as it had advanced; and it will not be denied that the shape of the face, the forehead, the eye, and the beard, are the most important features by which resemblance is determined.

'When the head had been entirely disengaged from the attachments which confined it, it was found to be loose, and without any difficulty was taken out and held up to view. The back part of the scalp was entirely perfect, and had a remarkably fresh appearance; the pores of the skin being more distinct, and the tendons and ligaments of the neck were of considerable substance and firmness. The hair was thick at the back part of the head, and in appearance nearly black. A portion of it, which has since been cleaned and dried, is of a beautiful dark brown color. That of the beard was a redder brown. On the back part of the head it was not more than an inch in length, and had probably been cut so short for the convenience of the executioner, or perhaps by the piety of friends soon after death, in order to furnish memorials of the unhappy king.

' On holding up the head, to examine the place of separation from the body, the muscles of the neck had evidently retracted themselves considerably; and the fourth cervical vertebra was found to be cut through its substance transversely, leaving the surfaces of the divided portions perfectly smooth and even, an appearance which could have been produced only by a heavy blow, inflicted with a very sharp instrument, and which furnished the last proof wanting to identify King Charles the First.'

The foregoing are two of the most successful instances of posthumous preservation. The care taken in regard to some other distinguished personages has been less fortunate in its result. The coffin of Henry VIII. was inspected at the same time with that of Charles, and was found to contain nothing but the mere skeleton of that king. Some portions of beard remained on the chin, but there was nothing to discriminate the personage contained in it.

During the present century, the sarcophagus of King John has also been examined. It contained little else than a disorganized mass of earth. The principal substances found, were some half decayed bones, a few vestiges of cloth and leather, and a long rusty piece of iron, apparently the remains of the sword-blade of that monarch.

The rapidity with which decomposition takes place in organic bodies, depends upon the particular circumstances under which they are placed. A certain temperature, and a certain degree of moisture, are indispensable agents in the common process of putrefaction, and could these be avoided in the habitable parts of our globe, human bodies might last indefinitely. I shall be excused for dwelling a short time on the influence of some of these preservative agents. Where a certain degree of cold exists, it tends powerfully to check the process of destructive fermentation, and when it extends so far as to produce congelation, its protecting power is complete. Bodies of men and animals are found in situations where they have remained frozen for years, and even for ages. Not many years ago, the bodies of some Spanish soldiers were found in a state of perfect preservation among the snows of the Andes, where they were supposed to have perished in attempting to cross those mountains, nearly a century ago; their costume and some historical records indicating the probable period of their expedition. At the Hospice of the Grand St. Bernard in the Alps, some receptacles of the dead are shown to travellers, in which, owing to the effect of perpetual frost, together with the lightness of the atmosphere, but little absolute decay has taken place in the subjects deposited during a lapse of years. But the most remarkable instance of preservation by frost of an animal body, is that of an elephant of an extinct species, discovered in 1806 in the ice of the polar sea, near the mouth of the river Lena, by Mr. Michael Adams. This animal was first seen by a chief of the Tonguse tribe, in the year 1799, at which time it was imbedded in a rock of ice about one hundred and eighty feet high, and had only two feet, with a small part of the body, projecting from the side, so as to be visible. At the close of the next summer, the entire flank of the animal had been thawed out. It nevertheless required five

summers, in this inclement region, to thaw the
ice, so that the whole body could be liberated.
At length, in 1804, the enormous mass separated
from the mountain of ice, and fell over upon its
side, on a sand bank. At this time it appears to
have been in a state of perfect preservation, with
its skin and flesh as entire as when it had existed
antecedently to the Deluge, or to whatever con-
vulsion of the globe may have transported animals,
apparently of the torrid zone, to the confines of
the Arctic circle. The Tonguse chief cut off the
tusks, which were nine feet long, and weighed
two hundred pounds each. Two years after this
event, Mr. Adams, being at Yakutsk, and hearing
of this event, undertook a journey to the spot.
He found the animal in the same place, but exceedingly mutilated by the dogs and wolves of
the neighborhood, which had fed upon its flesh as
fast as it thawed. He, however, succeeded in
removing the whole skeleton, and in recovering
two of the feet, one of the ears, one of the eyes,
and about three quarters of the skin, which was
covered with reddish hair and black bristles.
These are now in the museum at St. Petersburg.

The foregoing facts are sufficient to show that
a low degree of temperature is an effectual pre-

ventive of animal decomposition. On the other
hand, a certain degree of heat combined with a
dry atmosphere, although a less perfect protection,
is sufficient to check the destructive process.
Warmth, combined with moisture, tends greatly
to promote decomposition; yet if the degree of
heat, or the circumstances under which it acts,
are such as to produce a perfect dissipation of
moisture, the further progress of decay is arrested.
In the arid caverns of Egypt the dried flesh of
mummies, although greatly changed from its
original appearance, has made no progress towards ultimate decomposition, during two or three
thousand years. It is known that the ancient
Egyptians embalmed the dead bodies of their
friends, by extracting the large viscera from the
cavities of the head, chest, and abdomen, and filling them with aromatic and resinous substances,
particularly asphaltum, and enveloping the outside of the body in cloths impregnated with
similar materials. These impregnations prevented decomposition for a time, until perfect
dryness had taken place. Their subsequent
preservation, through so many centuries, appears
to have been owing, not so much to the anti-
septic quality of the substance in which they are

enveloped, as to the effectual exclusion of moisture.

In the crypt under the cathedral of Milan, travellers are shown the ghastly relics of Carlo Borromeo, as they have lain for two centuries, inclosed in a crystal sarcophagus, and bedecked with costly finery, of silk and gold. The preservation of this body is equal to that of an Egyptian mummy, yet a more loathsome piece of mockery than it exhibits can be hardly imagined.

It will be perceived that the instances which have been detailed are cases of extraordinary exemption, resulting from uncommon care, or from the most favorable combination of circumstances, such as can befall but an exceedingly small portion of the human race. The common fate of animal bodies is to undergo the entire destruction of their fabric, and the obliteration of their living features in a few years, and sometimes even weeks, after their death. No sooner does life cease, than the elements which constituted the vital body become subject to the common laws of inert matter. The original affinities, which had been modified or suspended during life, are brought into operation, the elementary atoms react upon each other, the organized structure passes into decay, and is converted to its original dust. Such is the natural, and, I may add, the proper destination of the material part of all that has once moved and breathed.

The reflections which naturally suggest themselves in contemplating the wrecks of humanity, which have occasionally been brought to light, are such as lead us to ask, of what possible use is a resistance to the laws of nature, which, when most successfully executed, can at best only preserve a defaced and degrading image of what was once perfect and beautiful? Could we, by any means, arrest the progress of decay, so as to gather round us the dead of a hundred generations in a visible and tangible shape; could we fill our houses and our streets with mummies, — what possible acquisition could be more useless, what custom could be more revolting? — For precisely the same reason the subterranean vaults and the walls of brick, which we construct to divide the clay of humanity from that of the rest of creation, and to preserve it separate for a time, as it were for future inspection, are neither useful, gratifying, nor ultimately effectual. Could the individuals themselves, who are to be the subjects of this care, have the power to regulate the officious zeal of their survivors, one of the last things they could reasonably desire would be, that the light should ever shine on their changed and crumbling relics.

On the other hand, when nature is permitted to take its course, when the dead are committed to the earth under the open sky, to become early and peacefully blended with their original dust, no unpleasant association remains. It would seem as if the forbidding and repulsive conditions which attend on decay, were merged and lost in the surrounding harmonies of the creation.

When the body of Major Andre was taken up, a few years since, from the place of its interment near the Hudson, for the purpose of being removed to England, it was found that the skull of that officer was closely encircled by a net-work, formed by the roots of a small tree, which had been planted near his head. This is a natural and most beautiful coincidence. It would seem as if a faithful sentinel had taken his post, to watch, till the obliterated ashes should no longer need a friend. Could we associate with inanimate clay any of the feelings of sentient beings, who would not wish to rescue his remains from the prisons of mankind, and commit them thus to the embrace of nature ?

Convenience, health, and decency require that the dead should be early removed from our sight. The law of nature requires that they should moulder into dust, and the sooner this change is accomplished, the better. This change should take place, not in the immediate contiguity of survivors, not in frequented receptacles provided for the promiscuous concentration of numbers, not where the intruding light may annually usher in a new tenant, to encroach upon the old. It should take place peacefully, silently, separately, in the retired valley, or the sequestered wood, where the soil continues its primitive exuberance, and where the earth has not become too costly to afford to each occupant at least his length and breadth.

Within the bounds of populous and growing cities, interments cannot with propriety take place beyond a limited extent. The vacant tracts reserved for burial grounds, and the cellars of churches which are converted into tombs, become glutted with inhabitants, and are in the end obliged to be abandoned, though not perhaps until the original tenants have been ejected, and the same space has been occupied three or four successive times. Necessity obliges a recourse at last

13

to be had to the neighboring country, and hence in Paris, London, Liverpool, Leghorn, and other European cities, cemeteries have been constructed without the confines of their population. These places, in consequence of the sufficiency of the ground, and the funds which usually grow out of such establishments, have been made the recipients of tasteful ornament. Travellers are attracted by their beauty, and dwell with interest on their subsequent recollection. The scenes which, under most other circumstances, are repulsive and disgusting, are by the joint influence of nature and art rendered beautiful, attractive, and consoling.

The situation of Mount Auburn, near Boston, is one of great natural fitness for the objects to which it has been devoted. Independently of its superior size, it may be doubted whether any spot, which has been set apart for the same purposes in Europe, possesses half the interest in its original features. In a few years, when the hand of taste shall have scattered among the trees, as it has already begun to do, enduring memorials of marble and granite, a landscape of the most picturesque character will be created. No place in the environs of our city will possess stronger attractions to the visitor. To the mourner it offers seclusion, amid the consoling influences of nature. The moralist and man of religion will

> ' Find room
> And food for meditation, nor pass by
> Much, that may give him pause, if pondered fittingly.'

We regard the relics of our deceased friends and kindred for what they have been, and not for what they are. We cannot keep in our presence the degraded image of the original frame; and if some memorial is necessary to soothe the unsatisfied want, which we feel when bereaved of their presence, it must be found in contemplating the place in which we know that their dust is hidden. The history of mankind, in all ages, shows that the human heart clings to the grave of its disappointed wishes, that it seeks consolation in rearing emblems and monuments, and in collecting images of beauty over the disappearing relics of humanity. This can be fitly done, not in the tumultuous and harassing din of cities, not in the gloomy and almost unapproachable vaults of charnel houses ; — but amidst the quiet verdure of the field, under the broad and cheerful light of heaven, — where the harmonious and ever changing face of nature reminds us, by its resuscitating influences, that to die is but to live again."

REPORT

Of the Garden and Cemetery Committee of the Massachusetts
Horticultural Society, at a meeting held on Saturday, September 17, 1834.

THE Garden and Cemetery Committee of the
Massachusetts Horticultural Society, beg leave
to submit the following Annual Report, for the
consideration of the Society : —

" The Committee congratulate the Society upon
the continued improvement of the Garden and
Cemetery, and the additional favor and encouragement, which the design has received from the
public. Before proceeding, however, to any particulars respecting this subject, they feel it their
duty to make a few remarks, in order to correct
some erroneous notions, which pervade certain
portions of the community, relative to the nature
and objects of the establishment. It is by no
means uncommon to find persons impressed with
the belief, that the establishment is a private speculation for the private benefit of the members of
the Society, or of the individuals, who originally
advanced the money to purchase the grounds for
the Garden and Cemetery, and that considerable
profits have been already realized from it. This

notion is utterly unfounded. The Cemetery is, in the truest and noblest sense, a public institution, that is, an institution of which the whole community may obtain the benefit upon easy and equal terms. No individual has any private interest in the establishment beyond what he acquires as the proprietor of a lot in the Cemetery; and every man in the community may become a proprietor upon paying the usual sum fixed for the purchase of a lot. The whole grounds are held by the Horticultural Society in trust for the purposes of a Garden and Cemetery; and no member thereof as such has any private interest therein, except as a corporator, or proprietor of a lot. The whole funds which have been already realized by the sale of lots have been devoted to paying the price of the original purchase, laying out the grounds, enclosing them with a fence, erecting an entrance gate and portal, and a cottage, and other structures for the accommodation of the superintendent, and defraying the incidental expenses. The expenditures have already amounted, asgappears by the Treasurer's Report, to upwards of twenty-five thousand dollars; and the proceeds of the sales have fallen short of this amount by about two thousand dollars; so that as yet the expenditures have exceeded the income. It has always been the understanding of the Society, that all the funds, which should be obtained by the sales of the lots, should, after defraying the annual expenses of the establishment, be applied exclusively to the preservation, repair, ornament, and permanent improvement of the Garden and Cemetery; and never to the private emolument of any of the members — and, indeed, this constituted the fundamental object of those, who have become the proprietors of lots. It is due also to the gentlemen, whose public spirit matured the design, to state, that it was their primary object to exclude all private speculation and interests from the undertaking; and, by a wise and fixed policy, to secure all the funds, which should arise from its success, to public purposes of an enduring and permanent character. The Society has sanctioned these views. It was believed that a generous community would foster the design; and, by a timely liberality, in the purchase of lots, would enable the Society to make this beautiful Retreat for the Dead at the same time the consolation and just pride of the Living. The Committee have great pleasure in stating that these reasonable expectations have not been disappointed. Mount Auburn has already become a place of general resort and interest, as well to strangers as to citizens; and its shades and paths, ornamented with monumental structures, of various beauty and elegance, have already given solace and tranquillizing reflections to many an afflicted heart, and awakened a deep moral sensibility in many a pious bosom. The Committee look forward, with increasing confidence, to a steady public patronage, which shall supply all the means necessary for the accomplishment of all the interesting objects of the establishment.

Relying on this patronage, the Committee indulge the hope that the period is not far distant, when, by the sale of lots, the Society will be enabled to enclose all the grounds with a permanent wall; to erect a Temple of simple and classical character, in which the service over the dead may be performed by clergymen of every denomination; to add extensively to the beauty and productiveness of the Garden; and, above all, to lay the foundation of an accumulating fund, the income of which shall be perpetually devoted to the preservation, embellishment, and improvement of the grounds. This last object the Com-

mittee deem of the highest importance to the
perpetuity of the establishment; and it cannot be
contemplated with too much care and earnestness
in all the future arrangements of the Society.
In addition to these objects, the Committee would
suggest the propriety of making arrangements
for the admission of water from Fresh Pond into
the ponds of the Cemetery ; and, after passing
through them, of conducting it into Charles River.
Such a measure would add to the salubrity of the
ponds, as well as improve the general aspect and
effect of the whole scenery. It is believed that
this measure may be accomplished at a comparatively small expense, whenever the funds of the
Society will admit of a suitable appropriation.
In the meantime it seems desirable to secure, by
some preliminary arrangement, the ultimate success of the project.

The Committee would further state, that by
the Report of the Treasurer it appears, that the
whole number of lots in the Cemetery, which
have been already sold, is 351, viz: —175 lots
in 1832, 76 lots in 1833, and 100 lots in 1834;
and the aggregate sum produced by these sales is
$23,225.72. The whole expenditures incurred
during the same years amount to $25,211.88.

The balance of cash and other available funds now in the hands of the Treasurer are $5403.32. The Committee are of opinion, that reliance may safely be placed upon the future sales of lots to defray the expenses of the current year; and that, therefore, a portion of the funds now on hand may be properly applied to the reduction of the remaining debts due by the Society.

The Committee would further state, that since the month of August, 1833, there have been ninety-three interments at Mount Auburn; eighteen tombs have been built; sixteen monuments have been erected; and sixty-eight lots have been turfed and otherwise ornamented. It is understood that other monuments are in progress, and will be erected in a short time.

The Committee would further state, that finding the grounds at Mount Auburn were visited by unusual concourses of people on Sundays, and that the injuries done to the grounds and shrubbery were far greater on those occasions than any other, circumstances which it is unnecessary to mention, they deemed it their duty, as well in reverence for the day, as in reference to the permanent interests of the establishment, and a regard to the feelings of the community, to make a regulation prohibiting any persons except proprietors and their families, and the persons accompanying them, from entering the grounds on Sundays. The effects of this regulation have been highly beneficial. It has not only given quiet to the neighborhood, and enabled proprietors and their families to visit their lots on Sundays under circumstances of more seclusion, tranquillity, and solemn religious feelings ; but it has put a stop to many of the depredations, which thoughtless and mischievous persons had been too apt to indulge in, in their recreations on that day. Several other regulations have been made, which experience had shown to be indispensable to the due security and uses of the Cemetery. The most important among these is the closing the gates at sunset and opening them at sunrise. And it may be observed of all these regulations, that while they allow a free access to the grounds to all visitors at reasonable times, and in a reasonable manner, they are calculated to prevent any desecration of them under false pretexts, or by secret misconduct.

The Committee would further state, that in pursuance of the vote of the Society, at their last annual meeting, they made an application to the

Legislature of the Commonwealth, at its last session, for additional provisions to aid the general objects of the Society. The Legislature accordingly passed an act, entitled 'An act in further addition to an act to incorporate the Massachusetts Horticultural Society,' which is entirely satisfactory to the Committee. They therefore beg leave to recommend, that the Society should, by a formal vote, accept the same.

All of which is respectfully submitted.

JOSEPH STORY, Chairman.

Sept. 20, 1834."

HYMN SUNG AT THE CONSECRATION.

WRITTEN BY THE REV. JOHN PIERPONT.

To thee, O GOD, in humble trust,
  Our hearts their cheerful incense burn,
For this thy word, " Thou art of dust,
  And unto dust shalt thou return."

For, what were life, life's work all done,
  The hopes, joys, loves, that cling to clay,
All, all, departed, one by one,
  And yet life's load borne on for aye !

Decay ! Decay ! 'tis stamped on all !
  All bloom, in flower and flesh, shall fade ;
Ye whispering trees, when we shall fall,
  Be our long sleep beneath your shade !

Here to thy bosom, mother Earth,
  Take back, in peace, what thou hast given ;
And all that is of heavenly birth,
  O GOD in peace, recall to heaven !

AN ACT

TO INCORPORATE THE PROPRIETORS OF THE CEMETERY AT MOUNT AUBURN.

1835.

Section 1. Be it enacted by the Senate and House of Representatives, in General Court assembled, and by the authority of the same, That Joseph Story, John Davis, Jacob Bigelow, Isaac Parker, George Bond, and Charles P. Curtis, together with such other persons as are proprietors of lots in the Cemetery at Mount Auburn, in the towns of Cambridge and Watertown, in the County of Middlesex, and who shall in writing signify their assent to this Act, their successors and assigns, be and they hereby are created a Corporation, by the name of the Proprietors of the Cemetery of Mount Auburn, and they shall have all the powers and privileges contained in the statute of the year one thousand eight hundred and thirty-three, chapter eighty-three.

Section 2.   Be it further enacted, That the said Corporation may take and hold in fee simple the Garden and Cemetery at Mount Auburn, *now held* by the Massachusetts Horticultural Society, and any other lands adjacent thereto, not exceeding fifty acres in addition to said Garden and Cemetery, upon the same trusts and for the same purposes, and with the same powers and privileges as the said Massachusetts Horticultural Society now hold the same by virtue of the statute of the year one thousand eight hundred and thirty-one, chapter sixty-nine; and may also take and hold any personal estate not exceeding in value fifty thousand dollars, to be applied to purposes connected with and appropriate to the objects of said establishment.

Section 3.   Be it further enacted, That all persons who shall hereafter become proprietors of lots in said Cemetery, of a size not less, each, than three hundred square feet, shall thereby become members of the said Corporation.

Section 4.   Be it further enacted, That the officers of the said Corporation shall consist of not less than seven nor more than twelve Trustees, a Treasurer, Secretary, and such other officers as they may direct. The Trustees shall be elected annually, at the annual meeting, and shall hold their offices until others are chosen. And they shall choose one of their number to be President, who shall be also President of the Corporation; and they shall also choose the Secretary and Treasurer, either from their own body or at large. And the said Trustees shall have the general management, superintendence, and care of the property, expenditures, business, and prudential concerns of the Corporation, and of the sales of lots in the said Cemetery, and they shall make a report of their doings to the Corporation at their annual meeting. The Treasurer shall give bonds for the faithful discharge of the duties of his office, and shall have the superintendence and management of the fiscal concerns of the Corporation, subject to the revision and control of the Trustees, to whom he shall make an annual report, which shall be laid before the Corporation at their annual meeting. And th Secretary shall be under oath for the faithful performance of the duties of his office, and shall record the doings at all meetings of the Corporation and of the Trustees.

Section 5. Be it further enacted, That the annual meetings of said Corporation shall be holden at such time and place as the by-laws shall direct, and the Secretary shall give notice thereof in one or more newspapers, printed in Boston, seven days at least before the time of meeting. And special meetings may be called by the Trustees in the same manner, unless otherwise directed by the by-laws; or by the Secretary, in the same manner, upon the written request of twenty members of the Corporation. At all meetings, a quorum for business shall consist of not less than seven members; and any business may be transacted, of which notice shall be given in the advertisements for the meeting, and all questions shall be decided by a majority of the members present, and voting either in person or by proxy.

Section 6. Be it further enacted, That as soon as the said Corporation shall have received from the Massachusetts Horticultural Society a legal conveyance of the said Garden and Cemetery at Mount Auburn, the Massachusetts Horticultural Society shall cease to have any rights, powers, and authorities over the same; and all the rights, powers, and authorities, trusts, immunities, and privileges conferred upon the said Society, and upon the proprietors of lots in the said Cemetery in and by virtue of the first section of the statute of the year one thousand eight hundred and thirty-one, chapter sixty-nine, shall be transferred to and exercised by the Corporation created by this Act; and the same shall, to all intents and purposes, apply to the said Corporation, and all proprietors of lots in the said Cemetery, with the same force and effect as if the same were herein specially enacted, and the said Corporation substituted for the Massachusetts Horticultural Society hereby.

Section 7. Be it further enacted, That any person who shall wilfully destroy, mutilate, deface, injure, or remove any tomb, monument, gravestone, or other structure placed in the Cemetery aforesaid, or any fence, railing, or other work for the protection or ornament of any tomb, monument, gravestone, or other structure aforesaid, or of any Cemetery lot, within the limits of the Garden and Cemetery aforesaid, or shall wilfully destroy, remove, cut, break, or injure any tree, shrub, or plant within the limits of the said Garden and Cemetery, or shall shoot or discharge any gun or other firearm within the said limits, shall be deemed guilty of a misdemeanor, and

14

shall, upon conviction thereof before any Justice of the Peace, or other court of competent jurisdiction within the county of Middlesex, be punished by a fine not less than Five Dollars nor more than Fifty Dollars, according to the nature and aggravation of the offence; and such offender shall also be liable, in an action of trespass, to be brought against him in any court of competent jurisdiction, in the name of the Proprietors of the Cemetery of Mount Auburn, to pay all such damages as shall have been occasioned by his unlawful act or acts; which money, when recovered, shall be applied by the said Corporation, under the direction of the Board of Trustees, to the reparation and restoration of the property destroyed or injured as above, and members of the said Corporation shall be competent witnesses in such suits.

Section 8. Be it further enacted, That the lots in said Cemetery shall be indivisible; and upon the death of any proprietor of any lot in the said Cemetery containing not less than three hundred square feet, the devisee of such lot, or the heir at law, as the case may be, shall be entitled to all the privileges of membership as aforesaid; and if there be more than one devisee or heir at law of each lot, the board of Trustees for the time being shall designate which of the said devisees or heirs at law shall represent the said lot, and vote in the meetings of the Corporation; — which designation shall continue in force, until by death, removal, or other efficient cause, another designation shall become necessary; and, in making such designation the Trustees shall, as far as they conveniently may, give the preference to males over females, and to proximity of blood and priority of age, having due regard, however, to proximity of residence.

Section 9. Be it further enacted, That it shall be lawful for the said Corporation to take and hold any grant, donation or bequest of property, upon trust, to apply the income thereof, under the direction of the board of Trustees, for the improvement or embellishment of the said Cemetery or of the Garden adjacent thereto, or of any buildings, structures, or fences erected or being erected upon the lands of the said Corporation, or of any individual proprietor of a lot in the Cemetery, or for the repair, preservation, or renewal of any tomb, monument, gravestone, fence, or railing, or other erection in or around any Cemetery lot, or for the planting and cultivation of trees, shrubs, flowers, or plants, in or around any Cemetery lot, according to the terms of such grant, donation, or bequest ; and the Supreme Judicial Court in this Commonwealth, or any other court therein having equity jurisdiction, shall have full power and jurisdiction to compel the due performance of the said trusts, or any of them, upon a bill filed by a proprietor of any lot in the said Cemetery for that purpose.

Section 10. Be it further enacted as follows : — First, That the present proprietors of lots in the said Cemetery, who shall become members of the Corporation created by this Act, shall henceforth cease to be members of the said Horticultural Society, so far as their membership therein depends on their being proprietors of lots in the said Cemetery. Secondly, That the sales of the Cemetery lots shall continue to be made as fast as it is practicable by the Corporation created by this Act, at a price not less than the sum of sixty dollars for every lot containing three hundred square feet, and so in proportion for any greater or less quantity, unless the said Horticultural Society and the Corporation created by this Act, shall mutually agree to sell the same at a less price. Thirdly, That the proceeds of the first

sales of such lots, after deducting the annual expenses of the Cemetery establishment, shall be
applied to the extinguishment of the present debts
due by the said Horticultural Society on account
of the said Garden and Cemetery. And after
the extinguishment of the said debts, the balance
of the said proceeds, and proceeds of all future
sales, shall annually, on the first Monday of every
year, be divided between the said Horticultural
Society and the Corporation created by this Act,
in manner following, namely: — Fourteen hundred dollars shall be first deducted from the gross
proceeds of the sales of lots during the preceding
year, for the purpose of defraying the Superintendent's salary and other incidental expenses of
the Cemetery establishment; and the residue of
the said gross proceeds shall be divided between
the said Horticultural Society and the Corporation
created by this Act, as follows, namely: — One
fourth part thereof shall be received by and paid
over to the said Horticultural Society, on the first
Monday of January of every year, and the remaining three fourth parts shall be detained and
held by the Corporation created by this Act, to
their own use forever. And if the sales of any
year shall be less than fourteen hundred dollars,

then the deficiency shall be a charge on the sales of the succeeding year or years.   Fourthly, The money so received by the said Horticultural Society shall be forever devoted and applied by the said Society to the purposes of an experimental garden, and to promote the art and science of Horticulture, and for no other purpose.   And the money so retained by the Corporation created by this Act, shall be forever devoted and applied to the preservation, improvement, embellishment, and enlargement of the said Cemetery and Garden, and the incidental expenses thereof, and for no other purpose whatsoever.   Fifthly, A Committee of the said Horticultural Society, duly appointed for this purpose, shall, on the first Monday of January of every year, have a right to inspect and examine the books and accounts of the Treasurer, or other officer acting as Treasurer of the Corporation created by this Act, as far as may be necessary to ascertain the sales of lots of the preceding year.

Section 11.   Be it further enacted, That any three or more of the persons named in this Act shall have authority to call the first meeting of the said Corporation, by an advertisement in one or more newspapers, printed in the City of Boston, seven days, at· least, before the time of holding such meeting, and specifying the time and place thereof. And all proprietors of lots, who shall before, at, or during the time of holding such meeting, by writing, assent to this Act, shall be entitled to vote in person or by proxy at the said first meeting. And at any such meeting or any such adjournment thereof, any elections may be had, and any business done, which are herein authorized to be had and done at an annual meeting, although the same may not be specified in the notice for the said meeting. And the first Board of Trustees, chosen at the said meeting, shall continue in office until the annual meeting of the said Corporation next ensuing their choice, and until another Board are chosen in their stead, in pursuance of this Act.

Section 12. Be it further enacted, That the said Cemetery shall be and hereby is declared exempted from all public taxes, so long as the same shall remain dedicated to the purposes of a Cemetery.

AN ACT IN ADDITION TO "AN ACT TO INCORPO-
RATE THE PROPRIETORS OF THE CEMETERY
OF MOUNT AUBURN."

1850.

BE it enacted by the Senate and House of
Representatives in General Court assembled, and
by the authority of the same, as follows:

The Corporation known as the Proprietors of
the Cemetery of Mount Auburn, may purchase
and hold in fee simple, or otherwise, any real
estate or any interest in any real estate situate
and lying in the towns of Cambridge and Watertown, in the County of Middlesex, anything in
the act of this Legislature passed March thirty-
first, A. D., eighteen hundred and thirty-five,
entitled "An Act to incorporate the Proprietors
of the Cemetery of Mount Auburn" — to the
contrary notwithstanding; *Provided always*, that
such real estate by the said Corporation so purchased, holden and possessed, as aforesaid, under
the provisions of this Act, shall not, at any one
time, exceed one hundred acres in extent, in addition to whatever the said Corporation now holds,
or is entitled to hold, by virtue of the Act to
which this Act is in addition as aforesaid.

AN ACT IN ADDITION TO AN ACT ENTITLED "AN ACT TO INCORPORATE THE MASSACHUSLTTS HORTICULTURAL SOCIETY."

1831.

Section 1. Be it enacted by the Senate and House of Representatives, in General Court assembled, and by the authority of the same, That the Massachusetts Horticultural Society be and hereby are authorized, in addition to the powers already conferred on them, to dedicate and appropriate any part of the real estate now owned or hereafter to be purchased by them, as and for a Rural Cemetery or Burying Ground, and for the erection of Tombs, Cenotaphs, or other Monuments, for or in memory of the dead : and for this purpose to lay out the same in suitable lots or other subdivisions, for family and other burying places ; and to plant and embellish the same with shrubbery, flowers, trees, walks, and other rural ornaments, and to enclose and divide the same with proper walls and enclosures, and to make and annex thereto other suitable appendages and conveniences, as the Society shall from time to time deem expedient. And whenever the said

Society shall so lay out and appropriate any of their real estate for a Cemetery or Burying Ground, as aforesaid, the same shall be deemed a perpetual dedication thereof for the purposes aforesaid ; and the real estate so dedicated shall be forever held by the said Society in trust for such purposes, and for none other. And the said Society shall have authority to grant and convey to any person or persons the sole and exclusive right of burial, and of erecting tombs, cenotaphs, and other monuments, in any such designated lots and subdivisions, upon such terms and conditions, and subject to such regulations as the said Society shall by their by-laws and regulations prescribe. And every right so granted and conveyed shall be held for the purposes aforesaid, and for none other, as real estate, by the proprietor or proprietors thereof, and shall not be subject to attachment or execution.

Section 2. Be it further enacted, That for the purposes of this Act, the said Society shall be and hereby are authorized to purchase and hold any real estate not exceeding ten thousand dollars in value, in addition to the real estate which they are now by law authorized to purchase and hold. And to enable the said Society more effect-

ually to carry the plan aforesaid into effect, and
to provide funds for the same, the said Society
shall be and hereby are authorized to open subscription books, upon such terms, conditions, and
regulations as the said Society shall prescribe,
which shall be deemed fundamental and perpetual articles between the said Society and the
subscribers. And every person who shall become
a subscriber in conformity thereto, shall be deemed
a member for life of the said Society without the
payment of any other assessment whatsoever ; and
shall moreover be entitled, in fee simple, to the
sole and exclusive right of using, as a place of
burial, and of erecting tombs, cenotaphs, and other
monuments, in such lot or subdivision of such
Cemetery or Burying Ground, as shall, in conformity to such fundamental articles, be assigned
to him.

Section 3. Be it further enacted, That the
President of the Society shall have authority to
call any special meeting or meetings of the said
Society, at such time and place as he shall direct,
for the purpose of carrying into effect any or all
the purposes of this Act, or any other purposes
within the purview of the original Act to which
this Act is in addition.

AN ACT IN ADDITION TO "AN ACT TO INCORPORATE THE PROPRIETORS OF THE CEMETERY OF MOUNT AUBURN."

BE it enacted by the Senate and House of Representatives in General Court assembled, and by the authority of the same, as follows:

Section 1. The Corporation known as the Proprietors of the Cemetery of Mount Auburn may grant and convey to the heirs at law, devisees, or trustees of any deceased person, any lot or lots, and additions to the same, in said Cemetery, for the purpose of burial, or of erecting tombs, cenotaphs, and other monuments, in and upon the same, to be held by the grantees in accordance with the provisions of Section Eight of the Act creating said Corporation.

Section 2. Said Corporation may grant and convey to any other corporate body, its successors and assigns, any lot or lots, and additions thereto, for the purposes aforesaid, which lot or lots, if containing more than three hundred square feet, may be represented by the president, treasurer, or such other officer as may be designated by such corporate body.

April 6th, 1859.

BY-LAWS.

THE code of By-laws contains regulations for the most part additional to, or explanatory of, those contained in the Act of Incorporation.

PROPRIETORS AND PRIVILEGES.

ART. 1. A proprietor holding not less than three hundred feet of land is a member of the Corporation, and, as such, is entitled to vote at meetings, and to hold a ticket admitting himself and his household to drive into the Cemetery. A proprietor holding less than three hundred feet is entitled to hold a like ticket of admission, but has not the right of voting.

MEETINGS.

ART. 2. The annual meeting of the Corporation shall be held in Boston, after due notification, on the first Monday in February, in the afternoon. At this meeting, the report of the Trustees for the preceding year shall be read, also the reports of the Treasurer and Superintendent. The Trustees for the ensuing year shall be elected by ballot, and other business specified in the advertisement may be transacted. If the Secretary neglect duly to call the annual meeting, a special meeting shall be called in the manner prescribed in the Act of Incorporation, and said special meeting shall be the annual meeting for the year in which it is held.

TRUSTEES AND OFFICERS.

ART. 3. The first meeting of the Trustees shall be called by the Secretary, and be held within two weeks after the annual meeting of the Corporation. At this meeting there shall be chosen by ballot, a President, Secretary, Treasurer, a Committee on Finance, a Committee on Lots, a Committee on Grounds, and a Committee on Regulations and Records of Interments, for the ensuing year. A Superintendent and Superintendent's Clerk, a Gate-keeper, and a Gardener, shall also be chosen by hand vote; and all salaries for the ensuing year shall be fixed. The Trustees shall meet at least once a month, and five Trustees shall constitute a quorum. No order of the Board, except to adjourn, shall be valid, unless it has received the votes of at least five Trustees.

The President shall call a special meeting of the Board, whenever requested in writing so to do by five Trustees.

No Trustee shall receive any salary, contract, or other emolument, for services rendered by him, while holding the office of Trustee; and neither the Superintendent, Gate-keeper, nor any other paid servant of the Corporation, shall have any interest whatever in any work or materials furnished for the Cemetery.

PRESIDENT.

ART. 4. The President shall preside at meetings of the Corporation and of the Trustees; he shall fix the time and place for special meetings; he shall nominate all committees not otherwise provided for; and shall report in writing at the annual meeting the doings of the Trustees for the preceding year. In the absence of the President, his place shall be supplied by a temporary chairman.

SECRETARY.

ART. 5. The Secretary shall notify and attend all meetings, and shall record the doings of the Corporation and of the Trustees. He shall prepare and superintend the advertisements and other publications of the Trustees and Corporation. He shall prepare all legal instruments, and shall give legal opinions on all subjects required by the Trustees. He shall have charge of the delivery of tickets, of Catalogues, and other publications of the Trustees. He shall prepare, countersign and record, in a book kept for the purpose, all deeds of conveyance of land in the Cemetery, and shall insert and keep in a portfolio, all plans duly made of lots for proprietors, and shall number the same, and keep an index by which they may conveniently be found.

The Secretary shall receive such salary as the Trustees may vote, together with the special fees designated for services to proprietors.

TREASURER.

ART. 6. The Treasurer shall give bonds in the sum of three thousand dollars for the faithful performance of the duties of his office. He shall have custody of the funds of the Corporation, under the direction of the Trustees. He shall collect dues and pay bills approved by the President, or by the chairman of any committee duly authorizing an expenditure. He shall keep the funds deposited in a bank to the credit of the Corporation, and draw the same as Treasurer. He shall sign all conveyances. He shall preserve and file all papers relating to his official duties, and shall report at the annual meeting the receipts and disbursements for the last year, and the existing state of the funds of the Corporation.

The Compensation of the Treasurer shall consist in a commission on sales, to be fixed annually by the Trustees.

SUPERINTENDENT.

ART. 7. The Superintendent shall reside near the Cemetery, and, under the direction of the Trustees, shall have the general care and custody thereof; shall keep the avenues, paths, and grounds in neat and satisfactory order; and, as agent for the Trustees, shall have the sole power to engage and discharge workmen on the ground, also to order and arrange their respective duties, and to pay their wages not otherwise provided for.

15

He shall see that the rights of the Corporation are respected by artists, mechanics, and laborers employed on the ground by individual proprietors. He shall see that all regulations with regard to interments and the construction of tombs be duly complied with. He shall fulfil all contracts made with proprietors for the repair of lots, and perform such other duties as the Trustees may require. He shall have the power to remove from the Cemetery improper and disorderly persons, also to abate nuisances, and remove rubbish and unnecessary incumbrances. He shall keep, in books provided for the purpose, regular and accurate records of all interments, including the names and ages of persons interred, and the place and date of their interment; also of all monuments erected, and lots inclosed, sodded, or otherwise improved; also of all moneys received or disbursed by him, whether for wages, fees, improvement of lots, sales of wood or other articles, purchases made, or services rendered. On the first day of every month, or oftener if required by the Trustees, he shall render to the Treasurer copies of said accounts, with proper vouchers, and pay over to him all moneys remaining in his hands. The compensation of the Superintendent shall be a salary, and the use of a house, with no other perquisites.

SUPERINTENDENT'S CLERK.

ART. 8. The Superintendent's Clerk shall assist the Superintendent by keeping the books, and performing such other duties as the Superintendent may require, and as are not incompatible with other duties required by the Trustees.

GATE-KEEPER.

ART. 9. The Gate-keeper shall attend the gate from sunrise to sunset, every day in the week, and see to the enforcement of the rules respecting admittance.

GARDENER.

ART. 10. The Gardener, under the direction of the Superintendent, shall take charge of and keep in repair, the lots of such proprietors as may apply to him for that service, and on such terms as may be agreed on between the parties; he shall also keep for sale at some convenient place designated by the Trustees, shrubs, trees, and flowers, and be ready to furnish, plant, or cultivate the same at his own expense, and for

such price and remuneration as may be agreed
on with the purchaser.

COMMITTEES.

ART. 11. Standing Committees shall be chosen by ballot, other Committees may be chosen by
hand vote. Vacancies occurring in any Committee shall be filled in the same manner as that
in which said Committee was chosen, and vacancies in Standing Committees shall be filled at a
meeting subsequent to that in which the vacancy
is announced. No Committee shall expend more
than one hundred dollars on any one object, unless
authorized so to do by vote of the Trustees.

COMMITTEE ON FINANCE.

ART. 12. The Committee on Finance shall
consist of two Trustees. They shall direct the
Treasurer in regard to all sales and all investments of the funds of the Corporation not otherwise provided for, or any part of the same. They
shall also act as auditors, and shall examine the
Treasurer's accounts before each annual meeting,
and satisfy themselves in regard to the correctness
of said accounts, also in regard to the safe preservation of all evidences of property belonging to

the Corporation ; and they shall annex their report to the annual report of the Treasurer.

COMMITTEE ON LOTS.

ART. 13. The Committee on Lots shall consist of three Trustees. They shall have the general supervision of all sales, locations, and enlargements of lots, also of all questions of right between individual proprietors, or between proprietors and the Corporation. No transfer or conveyance of land by the Corporation shall take place until it has received the approval, in writing, of a majority of the Committee on Lots. If an appeal to the Trustees is made by any party in interest, before the delivery of a deed, the Secretary shall delay acting until the case has been brought before the Trustees, and acted upon by them. The Committee on Lots shall have power, subject to the concurrence of the Trustees, to contract with any proprietor for the repair of his lot perpetually, or for an indefinite time. They shall at least twice in each year inspect the lots which the Trustees have undertaken to keep in repair, and see that the trust is duly executed.

COMMITTEE ON GROUNDS.

ART. 14. The Committee on Grounds shall consist of five Trustees. They shall have general charge of the grounds, trees, avenues, and paths in the Cemetery, with power to make such alterations, repairs, and improvements therein, as they shall deem expedient. But no avenues or paths shall be changed in situation, without the consent of the Trustees expressed by vote.

COMMITTEE ON REGULATIONS AND RECORDS OF INTERMENTS.

ART. 15. The Committee on Regulations and Records of Interments, shall consist of two Trustees. They shall superintend the general subject of interments, and see that the laws of the Commonwealth and those of the Cemetery, in relation thereto, be complied with. They shall, from time to time, inspect the records and accounts of the Superintendent, and see that the same are suitably kept.

INTERMENTS.

ART. 16. No interment shall be made at Mount Auburn until such a permit as may be required by the laws of the Commonwealth, or of the city or town from which the deceased may be brought, together with an order from the proprietor of the lot in which such interment is to be made, or from his legal representative, shall have been presented at the gate, nor until the fees shall have been paid.

Until otherwise ordered, two dollars and fifty cents shall be charged for digging a grave and making an interment, and fifty cents additional for recording the same. A deduction of one dollar shall be made from the above charges for a child under ten years of age. For each interment in a tomb, a charge shall be made by the Superintendent, according to the amount of service rendered in the case.

The particulars and amounts of fees for burial shall be printed on the back of the order from the proprietor, together with the words, " payable at the time of interment."

LOTS AND SPACES.

ART. 17. Lots shall be laid out by the Superintendent, subject to the approval of the Committee on Lots. In all future sales of lots, a space of not less than three nor more than six feet in width, at the discretion of the Committee on Lots, shall be reserved between the fence limits of different lots, unless otherwise ordered by vote of the Trustees.

The land left vacant as intermediate 'space between lots in Mount Auburn, and not exceeding ten feet in width between any two lots, may be sold to the nearest lot holder or holders, at one third of the selling prices per foot at the time of said sale, with the condition that said land shall forever be kept open and without interments: provided that, if the Committee on Lots deem it inexpedient in any special case to make such sale, the question may be submitted to the Board of Trustees.

The price of a full lot, until otherwise ordered, shall be one hundred and fifty dollars, or fifty cents per square foot. Enlarged lots, small lots, and land additional to lots, will be sold at a corresponding rate per foot. Choice lots in such places as the Trustees may designate, will be held at an advanced price.

No lots shall be gratuitously conveyed to public bodies or private individuals.

PUBLIC LOTS.

ART. 18. Interments may be made in the public lots belonging to the Cemetery, and the graves numbered on stone, on payment of twelve dollars each, together with the customary fees payable in other cases of interment; but no slab, monument, or fence shall be erected upon or around said graves without the approval of the Committee on Lots; and, in case the body thus interred is removed from the Cemetery, the right is thereby vacated, and no allowance is made by the Corporation.

SALES AND CONVEYANCES.

ART. 19. Lots applied for by purchasers shall be laid out by the Superintendent, subject to the approval of the Committee on Lots. Upon the selection of a lot, the Superintendent shall issue to the party intending to purchase a certificate, giving him a right to pay for the lot at any time within five days, if the sale shall be approved by the Committee on Lots; otherwise the bargain for sale shall be void. If the sale is approved by a majority of said Committee, the purchaser shall then pay to the Treasurer the customary or stipulated price of the lot sold him, and the Secretary's fee of one dollar, and receive a certificate therefor. The Secretary, on receiving the Treasurer's order for the deed of said lot, shall make, record, and return said deed to the Treasurer, who will deliver the same to the purchaser, upon his presenting the certificate, and receipting for said deed. In any doubtful case the Secretary or Treasurer shall ask instruction from the Trustees before executing a deed.

No deed of any lot shall be issued to more than one grantee ; nor to any person as trustee, executor, or administrator, except by the vote of the Trustees, or the authority of the Committee on Lots. This rule is not to apply to heirs at law, devisees, or trustees of a deceased person, or to a corporate body, in accordance with a provision of the Legislature of Massachusetts, passed April 6th, 1859. No deed of any lot shall contain any *special* declaration of trust, without a vote of the Trustees therefor.

All deeds of conveyance by the Corporation shall be under the common seal, which shall be that heretofore adopted ; and signed by the Treasurer, and countersigned by the Secretary, and recorded in the books of the Corporation. One dollar shall be paid to the Secretary for recording any deed of transfer, and giving the due certificate of the same.

The forms of conveyance given in Appendix A, shall be used until otherwise ordered by the Trustees.

LOTS OF DECEASED PROPRIETORS.

ART. 20. When the devisee of a deceased proprietor of any lot in the Cemetery shall desire to place upon the record of the deed of said lot, at the Secretary's office, the evidence of his title to the same, he may do so by producing a certified copy of the will of such proprietor (if the title is deducible therefrom), or of such portion of said will as relates to said title; and the same shall be duly recorded in a book kept for that purpose, and proper reference thereto be made upon the margin of the original record. The Secretary shall receive the affidavit of any person who shall claim to be the sole heir at law of the deceased proprietor of any lot, in which the material facts necessary to support such claim shall be set forth, and he shall file the same with the papers of the Corporation, with proper reference thereto, upon the margin of the original record.

When the devisees or heirs at law of any deceased proprietor, or the guardian or trustee of such persons being infants, shall desire the appointment of a person to represent the lot owned in common by them, written application to the Trustees shall be made by them in that behalf. Any person who shall be designated by any company, society, or association, whether corporate or incorporate, which may own a lot of three hundred feet or more in the Cemetery, is authorized to represent such lot and vote at the meetings of the Corporation. Lots of less than three hundred square feet may be represented in the same manner as other lots for all purposes not conflicting with the charter.

PLANS AND PORTFOLIOS.

ART. 21. A large map or plan of the Cemetery shall be kept at the Secretary's office, and a duplicate of the same at the Superintendent's office. On these shall be entered, under the direction of the Committee on Lots, by a surveyor to be from time to time designated by them, all avenues and paths duly named, and all lots sold or laid out by the Corporation duly numbered. If any avenue, path, or lot shall be given up, altered, or removed by the Trustees, a corresponding alteration shall be made in the plan.

The Secretary shall procure and keep one or more portfolios, in which he shall insert such plans as proprietors may respectively procure to be made of their lots, such plans to be drawn by a surveyor approved by the Trustees, on paper of uniform size, which shall be furnished by the Secretary, and no plans shall be introduced into the portfolio unless they shall have been examined and approved by the Committee on Lots, or a majority of them, and certified by the Superintendent to be correct. Proprietors shall pay the expense of their own plans, and one dollar to the Secretary for examining and introducing the same into the portfolio and placing the name in the index.

TREES.

ART. 22. Trees standing within lots can be removed, if desired, by an application from the proprietor to the Superintendent, subject to the approval of the Committee on Grounds. The Committee on Grounds have likewise charge of the general subject of introducing and cultivating, also of trimming and removing trees and shrubs in other parts of the Cemetery.

TOMBS.

ART. 23. Lots for tombs may be sold in places approved by the Trustees, and at prices fixed by them. Such tombs shall be made in a strong, tight, and durable manner, and, except in catacombs,—made as hereinafter described,— every part, including the door, shall be at least one foot under ground.

CATACOMBS.

ART. 24. Catacomb tombs may be constructed in such places and manner as shall be approved by the Committee on Lots, with the entrance doors above ground ; but no bodies shall be placed in them, except in single compartments made satisfactory to the Superintendent, and closed so as to be hermetically tight, with brick or stone and cement.

RECEIVING TOMBS.

ART. 25. Bodies may be deposited in the receiving tombs on payment of twenty dollars to the Superintendent or Treasurer. But if within four months after interment, the deposited body shall be removed to any part of Mount Auburn, fifteen dollars of the above sum shall be refunded, otherwise the whole twenty dollars shall be forfeited to the Corporation ; and the Superintendent shall remove the body to such place as shall be directed by the Committee on Grounds. But the friends or relatives, with the consent of the Superintendent, and in a legal way, may, at their own expense, remove said body from the Cemetery.

MONUMENTS, STONES, FENCES, ETC.

ART. 26. Proprietors have the right to erect on their lots, fences, monuments, and stones, of appropriate character. Wooden fences and gravestones of slate are not permitted. Live hedges of small or moderate size are allowed. All foundations of monuments and other structures shall be made satisfactory to the Superintendent, under the direction of the Committee on Lots.

APPROPRIATIONS.

ART. 27. No appropriation of money exceeding one thousand dollars for any one object, unless it be for the liquidation of a debt previously existing, shall be made by the Trustees, except at a meeting at least seven days subsequent to the meeting in which the said appropriation has been moved; whereof special notice shall have been given.

COLLECTION AND PAYMENT OF MONEY.

ART. 28.   All sums due the Corporation of one hundred dollars and upwards shall be paid to the Treasurer; and all bills of like amount shall be paid by him; and all bills except those for labor shall be approved either by the proprietor for whom the work is done, or by the Committee on Lots; provided that nothing herein contained shall be understood as conflicting with the provisions of any existing by-laws.

REPAIR FUND.

ART. 29.   The Trustees will receive in trust from any proprietor, a sum of money not less than one hundred dollars, the income of which shall be appropriated to the repair of his lot, according to the terms of trust given in the Appendix.

The Trustees may also *guarantee* the perpetual repair of lots, containing three hundred feet and upwards, on the payment to the Treasurer of a sum not less than three hundred dollars, and of lots containing less than three hundred feet, on the payment of a sum not less than one hundred dollars, according to the terms of trust given in the Appendix. In this case, if the Repair Fund should ever be lost, the whole property of the Corporation is held for the perpetual repair of such lots.

All monies received from proprietors, for the purpose of keeping lots in repair, shall collectively constitute a separate fund, to be called the " Repair Fund," and shall be kept invested, under the direction of the Committee on Finance, in some public stock of this State, or of the National Government, or in the stock of some bank or banks of this State, or in some personal notes or obligations of private persons, secured by a satisfactory collateral pledge, or mortgage on interest.

Each lot, in relation to which such contract shall have been made, shall be credited in a book kept for the purpose, with the principal sum given on account of said lot, and at the close of each year, a ratable proportion of the net income of the whole Repair Fund, less one half per cent., shall be carried to the credit of each lot, and the proper entries made accordingly.

The Treasurer shall keep the Superintendent constantly informed as to all lots which the Corporation have agreed to keep in repair, and shall

16

also state the sums paid by the proprietors as consideration for such agreements.

A list of the lots, the repair of which has been contracted for by the Corporation, shall be published in each edition of the Catalogue of proprietors, together with the names of the present owners, and the sums respectively paid on said lots.

ADMITTANCE.

ART. 30. The Secretary shall furnish to each proprietor who may request it, a ticket, entitling him and his household to drive with a carriage into the Cemetery. These tickets are not transferable.

In all cases where the Secretary is satisfied, by a written petition to the Trustees, that the heirs or devisees in common of any lot have agreed upon any one person to represent the same, he may issue the ticket for such lot to the person designated in such petition as representative of such lot, to remain good until the further action of the Board. The petition, however, shall be presented, with notice of the Secretary's action, at the next meeting of the Trustees.

The Secretary is authorized to issue more than

one ticket upon one lot, where he is satisfied that two or more persons are actual owners of a lot in fact, though the title is in the name of one only.

The Secretary is authorized to replace tickets which he is satisfied are actually lost. But if the lost ticket is found, the duplicate shall be returned to the Secretary.

Strangers from a distance, also persons having business in the Cemetery, may be admitted with carriages on presenting a note or ticket of admission signed by a Trustee or by the Secretary or Treasurer. The Trustees, however, may from time to time pass such votes for the admission of strangers and other non-proprietors, and under such regulations as they may deem expedient.

The public are, at present, allowed to walk into the Cemetery, except on Sundays and holidays. Persons having a relative or near friend interred there, may enter the Cemetery on Sundays and holidays, on presenting a card of admission from a Trustee, the Secretary, or Treasurer. All visitors are subject to the conditions and regulations prescribed in the by-laws.

Teams, carts, and heavy loaded vehicles are not allowed to enter the front gate without the order of a Trustee. No omnibuses are allowed to enter the Cemetery.

The rules and regulations concerning visitors to the Cemetery shall be as given in the Appendix until otherwise ordered by the Trustees.

FUNERALS.

ART. 31. Early notice of funerals should be given to the Superintendent on the ground at Mount Auburn. When a funeral arrives, a person will be in readiness at the gate to conduct the procession to the place of interment. If military funerals on foot or on horseback are admitted, no music nor firing of volleys will be allowed within the Cemetery.

ALTERATIONS OF BY-LAWS.

ART. 32. No alteration nor addition shall be made in any of the By-laws, unless the proposed alteration or addition shall have been submitted to the Trustees at a meeting at least seven days previous to the meeting at which it is to be acted upon.

APPENDIX.

FORM FOR CONVEYANCE OF LOTS.

KNOW ALL MEN BY THESE PRESENTS, That the Proprietors of the Cemetery of Mount Auburn, in consideration of   dollars,   paid to them by   of   the receipt of which is hereby acknowledged, do hereby grant, bargain, sell, and convey to the said   and   heirs and assigns, one lot of land in the Cemetery of Mount Auburn, in the County of Middlesex, situated on the way called   and numbered, on the plan of said Cemetery,   which plan is in the possession of the said Corporation, for inspection by the said grantee,   heirs and assigns, at all seasonable times, the said lot of land containing   superficial square feet.

To have and to hold the aforegranted premises unto the said   heirs and assigns, forever; subject, however, to the conditions and limitations, and with the privileges following, to wit :

First. That the proprietor of the said lot shall have the right to enclose the same, with a wall or fence not exceeding one foot in thickness, which may be placed on the adjoining land of the Corporation, exterior to the said lot.

Second. That the said lot of land shall not be used for

any other purpose than as a place of burial for the dead; and no trees within the lot or border, shall be cut down or destroyed, without the consent of the Trustees of the said Corporation.

Third. That the proprietor of the said lot shall have the right to erect stones, monuments or sepulchral structures, and to cultivate trees, shrubs, and plants in the same.

Fourth. The proprietor of the said lot of land shall erect, at his or her own expense, suitable landmarks of stone or iron, at the corners thereof; and shall also cause the number thereof to be legibly and permanently marked on the premises. And if the said proprietor shall omit, for thirty days after notice, to erect such landmarks, and mark the number, the Trustees shall have authority to cause the same to be done at the expense of the said proprietor.

Fifth. That if the landmarks and boundaries of the said lot shall be effaced, so that the said lot cannot, with reasonable diligence, be found and identified, the said Trustees shall set off to the said grantee,   heirs or assigns, a lot in lieu thereof, in such part of the Cemetery as they see fit, and the lot hereby granted shall, in such case, revert to the Corporation.

Sixth. That if any trees or shrubs situated in said lot of land shall, by means of their roots, branches, or otherwise, become detrimental to the adjacent lots or avenues, or dangerous or inconvenient to passengers, it shall be the duty of the said Trustees, for the time being, and they shall have the right, to enter into the said lot and remove the said trees and shrubs, or such parts thereof as are thus detrimental, dangerous, or inconvenient.

Seventh. That if any monument or effigy, or any structure whatever, or any inscription be placed in or upon the said land, which shall be determined by the major part of the said Trustees for the time being, to be offensive or improper, the said Trustees, or the major part of them, shall have the right, and it shall be their duty, to enter upon said land, and remove the said offensive or improper object or objects.

Eighth. No fence shall, from time to time or at any time, be placed or erected in or around the said lot, the materials and design of which shall not first have been approved by the Trustees, or a committee of them.

Ninth. No tomb shall be constructed within the bounds of the Cemetery, except in or upon the lots situated in such parts of the grounds as shall be designated by the Trustees for that purpose; and no proprietor shall suffer the remains of any person to be deposited in a tomb so authorized, *for hire.*

Tenth. The said lot of land shall be holden subject to the provisions contained in an act of the General Court, dated March 31, 1835, and entitled "An Act to incorporate the Proprietors of the Cemetery of Mount Auburn."

And the said Proprietors of the Cemetery of Mount Auburn do hereby covenant to and with the said   heirs and assigns, that they are lawfully seised of the aforegranted premises, and of the ways leading to the same from the highway, in fee simple; that they are free from all incumbrances; that the Corporation have a right to sell and convey the said premises to the said   for the purposes above expressed; and that they will warrant and defend the same unto the said   heirs and assigns forever.

And the said Proprietors of the Cemetery of Mount Auburn further covenant to and with the said   heirs and assigns, that the provisions of an order passed by the Trustees of this Corporation, on the sixth day of April, in the year eighteen hundred and fifty-seven, (which is made part of this covenant, as if herein repeated,) for the establishment and security of a fund for the preservation of the Cemetery and its appurtenances, shall' be forever kept, observed, and performed by the said Corporation.

In testimony whereof, the said Proprietors of the Cemetery of Mount Auburn have caused this instrument to be signed by their Treasurer and countersigned by their Secretary, and their Common Seal to be hereto affixed, the day of   in the year of our Lord one thousand eight hundred and

---

FORM FOR CONVEYANCE OF SPACES BETWEEN LOTS, TO BE KEPT OPEN.

KNOW ALL MEN BY THESE PRESENTS, That the Proprietors of the Cemetery of Mount Auburn, in consideration of   dollars, paid to them by   of   the receipt of which is hereby acknowledged, do hereby grant, bargain, sell, and convey to the said   and   heirs and assigns, a certain piece of land in the Cemetery of Mount Auburn, adjoining the   side of   lot, which is situated on the way called   and numbered   on the plan of said Cemetery; the said piece of land being   feet wide   and   feet in length, containing   square feet.

To Have and to Hold the aforegranted premises unto the said   heirs and assigns forever; subject, however, to the conditions and limitations following, to wit:

First. That no part of said premises shall ever be used as a place of burial for the dead; unless the owner of the said lot shall purchase the same for the purpose of enlarging his burial lot.

Second. That the whole of said premises shall forever remain as a part of the open grounds of said Cemetery; except in the event of being purchased by the owner of the said lot as aforesaid.

Third. That no tree, shrub, or plant, and no inscription, landmark, monument, fence, or structure whatever, shall be placed in or upon the premises, or be removed therefrom, without the consent of the Board of Trustees, for the time being, of said Corporation.

And the said Proprietors of the Cemetery of Mount Auburn do hereby covenant to and with the said heirs and assigns, that they are lawfully seised of the aforegranted premises, and of the ways leading to the same from the highway, in fee simple; that they are free from all incumbrances; that the Corporation have a right to sell and convey the said premises to the said for the purposes above expressed; and that they will warrant and defend the same unto the said heirs and assigns forever.

And the said Proprietors of the Cemetery of Mount Auburn further covenant to and with the said heirs and assigns, that the provisions of an order passed by the Trustees of this Corporation, on the sixth day of April, in the year eighteen hundred and fifty-seven, (which is made part of this covenant, as if herein repeated,) for the establishment and security of a fund for the preservation of the Cemetery and its appurtenances, shall be forever kept, observed, and performed by the said Corporation.

In testimony whereof, the said Proprietors of the Cemetery of Mount Auburn have caused this instrument to be signed by their Treasurer and countersigned by their Secretary, and their Common Seal to be hereto affixed, the day of in the year of our Lord one thousand eight hundred and

FORM FOR DONATION IN TRUST FOR THE RE-PAIR OF LOTS.

BE IT KNOWN, that I,   of
the Proprietor of Lot No.   in the Cemetery of
Mount Auburn, do hereby give unto the Proprietors of the
Cemetery of Mount Auburn, the sum of
        dollars, for their sole use forever ; in trust, neverthe-
less, that the Trustees of the said Corporation for the time
being, shall, in order to obtain an income therefrom, invest
the same from time to time, in their discretion, in some
public stock of this State, or of the National Government,
or in the stock of some Bank or Banks of this State, or in
some personal notes or obligations of private persons, secured by a satisfactory collateral pledge or mortgage, on
interest, and to apply the income or interest thereof, from
time to time, after deducting therefrom the sum of fifty
cents out of every hundred dollars of the sum so above
given, as follows : —

First. To keep in suitable and good repair and preservation, Lot No.   in the said Cemetery, and the
monument, fences, trees, shrubbery, and soil thereon.

Secondly. To suffer the surplus, if any, of such income
or interest to accumulate for such time as the said Trustees
may deem expedient, or in their discretion to apply the
same surplus, or any part thereof, from time to time, to the
ornament and preservation of the grounds of the said Cemetery, or to any other, or all the purposes to which, by the
Act of Incorporation, the funds of the said Corporation
may be lawfully applied, and which are appropriate to the
objects of the establishment of said Cemetery.

Provided, however, That the said Trustees shall never be
responsible for their conduct in the premises, except for
good faith and such reasonable diligence as may be required
of mere gratuitous agents ; and *provided further,* that the

said Trustees shall in no case be obliged to make any separate investment of the sum so given, and that the average income or interest derived from all funds of the like nature belonging to the Corporation, shall be divided annually, and carried proportionally to the credit of each lot entitled thereto.

In witness whereof, I have hereunto set my hand and seal, on this   day of
A D 18

Executed in presence of

FORM FOR DONATION IN TRUST FOR PERPETUAL REPAIR OF LOTS.

[The same as preceding, with the following clause, inserted immediately after the *in testimonium* clause.]

MOUNT AUBURN CEMETERY.

The Committee on Lots hereby certify that they approve of the sum of   dollars as sufficient to warrant the guaranty on the part of the Proprietors of the Cemetery of Mount Auburn, that the within named Lot numbered   shall be forever kept in good order and repair.

Committee on Lots, A. D. 18

N B. — Printed blanks for donation in trust for the care of Lots, in the foregoing forms, are gratuitously furnished by the Secretary to proprietors who may request them.

REGULATIONS CONCERNING VISITORS TO THE CEMETERY.

The gates are opened at sunrise, and closed at sunset.

No money is to be paid to the Gatekeeper.

No persons are admitted on SUNDAYS or HOLIDAYS, except PROPRIETORS and members of their HOUSEHOLD, and persons accompanying them.

No refreshments, and no party carrying refreshments, will be admitted to come within the grounds at Mount Auburn.

All persons who shall be found within the grounds making unseemly noises, or otherwise conducting themselves unsuitably to the purposes to which the grounds are devoted, will be required instantly to leave the grounds, and upon refusal will be compelled to do so; such persons will also be prosecuted.

No vehicle is to be driven, in the Cemetery, *at a rate faster than a walk.*

No horse is to be left unfastened without a keeper.

No horse is to be fastened, except at the posts provided for this purpose.

All persons are prohibited from gathering any flowers, EITHER WILD OR CULTIVATED, or breaking any tree, shrub, or plant.

Any person who shall be found in possession of flowers or shrubs, while in the grounds, or before leaving them, will be deemed to have unlawfully taken them in the grounds, and will be prosecuted accordingly. N. B. — Persons carrying flowers INTO the Cemetery, to be placed on any lot or grave, as offerings or memorials, are requested to notify the Gatekeeper, as they pass in ; in every other case flowers brought to the Cemetery *must be left without the gate, or with the Gatekeeper,* until the owner passes out again.

All persons are prohibited from writing upon, defacing, and injuring any monument, fence, or other structure, in or belonging to the Cemetery.

All persons are prohibited from discharging fire-arms in the Cemetery.

The Superintendent, the Gatekeeper, and any other person acting under them, shall have a right to require his or her name, from any person other than a proprietor, or a member of his family, who shall visit the grounds, and upon his or her refusal, or giving a false name, to exclude them from the grounds.

The Superintendent, the Gatekeeper, and all other persons acting under them, shall have full authority to carry these regulations into effect, and shall give notice of any violations thereof to the Trustees.

☞ The Superintendent has the care of the Cemetery, and is authorized to remove all those who violate these regulations, or commit trespasses. Trespassers are also liable to be fined FIFTY DOLLARS.

☞ TWENTY DOLLARS reward is offered to any person who shall give information to the Trustees, which shall lead to the conviction of the offender, of any trespass done by taking or plucking any flowers, shrubs, or trees, within the grounds, or of otherwise injuring the grounds, or of any other offence against the laws and regulations provided for the protection of the Cemetery, and the monuments and erections therein.

OFFICERS FROM 1831 TO 1860.

PRESIDENTS.

Joseph Story,	from 1835 to 1845	
Jacob Bigelow,	" 1845 " 1860	

SECRETARIES.

George W. Pratt,	" 1831 " 1832	
Charles P. Curtis,	" 1832 " 1835	
Benjamin R. Curtis,	" 1835 " 1844	
Henry M. Parker,	" 1844 " 1855	
Austin J. Coolidge,	" 1855 " 1860	

TREASURERS.

George Bond,	" 1831 " 1842	
George W. Bond,	" 1842 " 1860	

SUPERINTENDENTS

David Haggerston	" 1832 " 1834	
John W. Russell,	" 1833 " 1840	
Rufus Howe,	" 1840 " 1855	
Jonathan Mann,	" 1855 " 1860	

GARDENER.

Anthony Apple,	" 1858 " 1860	

TRUSTEES.

Joseph Story,	" 1831 " 1845	
Jacob Bigelow,	" 1831 " 1860	
George Bond,	" 1831 " 1842	
Benjamin A Gould,	" 1831 " 1859	
H. A. S. Dearborn,	" 1831 " 1833	
George W. Brimmer,	" 1831 " 1832	

Charles Wells . . . . from 1831 to 1832
Zebedee Cook, Jr. . . . . " 1832 " 1833
Edward Everett, ... " 1831 " 1832
George W. Pratt, ... " 1831 " 1832
Joseph P. Bradlee, . . . " 1833 " 1837
Charles Brown, ... " 1833 " 1837
Charles P. Curtis, . . . " 1833 " 1860
Samuel Appleton, . . . " 1834 " 1837
Elijah Vose, ... " 1834 " 1835
James Read, ... " 1835 " 1860
Benjamin R. Curtis, . . . " 1837 " 1851
Martin Brimmer, . . . " 1838 " 1847
Isaac Parker, ... " 1838 " 1854
Samuel T. Armstrong, . . " 1839 " 1840
George W. Crockett, . . . " 1843 " 1855
John C. Gray, ... " 1845 " 1849
John J. Dixwell, ... " 1847 " 1851
Mace Tisdale, ... " 1850 " 1858
George H. Kuhn, . . . " 1852 " 1855
Charles C. Little, . . . " 1852 " 1860
Isaiah Bangs, . . . " 1854 " 1859
James Cheever, ... " 1856 " 1860
Uriel Crocker, ... " 1856 " 1860
William R. Lawrence, . . " 1856 " 1860
Henry S. McKean, . . . " 1856 " 1857
Charles G. Nazro, . . . " 1856 " 1860
William T. Andrews, . . . " 1859 " 1860
Jacob Sleeper, ... " 1859 " 1860
Edward Tobey, . . . " 1859 " 1860

Before 1835 the Board acting as Trustees were called the
" Garden and Cemetery Committee."

DIRECTORY TO AVENUES AND PATHS.

17

Rosebay   leads from Larch across the bridge to same.
Spruce   "   "   Pine to Fir, thence by westerly side of
        Cemetery to Walnut.
Walnut   "   "   Central Square to Mountain.
Willow   "   "   Poplar to Larch.
Yew   "   "   Garden to Ash.

PATHS.

Acacia   leads from Spruce Av. to Verbena P.
Acanthus   "   "   Larch to Magnolia Av.
Acorn   "   "   Maple Av. to Evergreen P.
Ailanthus lies between Central, Cypress, and Cedar Avs.
Alder   leads from Locust to Poplar Av.
Almond   "   "   Indian Ridge P. to the same.
Aloe   "   "   Indian Ridge P. to Lime Av.
Althæa   "   "   Maple to Garden Pond.
Amaranth encircles the crown of Harvard Hill.
Anemone   leads from Spruce Av. to Orange P.
Andromeda   "   "   Maple to Garden Pond.
Arbutus   "   "   Lime Av. to
Arethusa   "   "   Walnut Av. to Trefoil P.
Asclepias   "   "   Spruce to Fir Av.
Asphodel   "   "   Lawn to Chapel Av.
Aster   "   "   Vine to Ivy P.
Azalea   "   "   Spruce Av. to same.
Bellwort   "   "   Spruce Av. to Orange P.
Buckthorn   "   "   Oak to Citron Av.
Camellia   "   "   Yew to Maple Av.
Catalpa   "   "   Indian Ridge P. to same.
Columbine   "   "   Spruce to Fir Av.
Cowslip   "   "   Spruce to Walnut Av.
Clethra   "   "   Yew to Maple Av.
Daisy   "   "   Locust Av. to Alder P.
Dell   "   "   Vine P., on East and west sides of
        Pond to S. side, thence to Ivy P.
Elder   "   "   Walnut to Spruce Av.
Eglantine   "   "   Fir to Spruce Av.
Evergreen   "   "   Lime Av. to same.

Fern	leads from Mountain to Walnut Av
Gentian	" " Cypress to Pine and Spruce Avs.
Geranium lies between Central and Beech Avs.
Green Brier	leads from Pine Av. to Mistletoe P.
Harebell	" " Walnut Av. to Trefoil P.
Hawthorn	" " Chestnut Av., by two ways, to Sweet Briar P.
Hazel	" " Mountain Av. to Rose P.
Heath	leads from Spruce to Fir Av.
Heliotrope	" " Spruce to Fir Av.
Hemlock	" " Poplar Av. to Ivy P.
Hibiscus lies between Cypress and Cedar Avs., entrance and exit on Cypress.
Honeysuckle	leads from Green Briar P. to St. John's Lot
Holly	" " Poplar Av. to Ivy P.
Hyacinth	" " Cypress to Chapel Av.
Indian Ridge	" " Central to Larch and Maple Avs
Iris	" " Moss to Ivy P.
Ivy	" " Central Square to Woodbine P.
Jasmine	" " Chestnut Av. to Hawthorn P
Kalmia	" " Yew to Maple Av.
Laburnum	" " Spruce Av. near Lawn to Chapel.
Lavender	" " Mountain to Chestnut
Lilac	" " Willow Av. to Indian Ridge P.
Lily	" " Poplar Av. to Aster P., thence to Woodbine P.
Linden	" " Beech Av. to same.
Lupine	" " Cypress to Spruce Av.
Mimosa	" " Spruce to Fir Av.
Mistletoe	" " Elm Av. to St. John's Lot, thence to Fir Av.
Moss	" " Laurel Av. to Ivy P.
Myrtle	" " Chestnut Av. to Hazel P.
Narcissus	" " Willow Av. to Catalpa P., and around Forest Pond back to Willow Av.
Oleander	" " Myrtle to Rose P.
Olive	" " Myrtle to Sweet Brier P.
Orange	" " Walnut Av. to same.

Orchis	leads from	Walnut Av. to Tulip P.
Osier	" "	Willow Av. to Indian Ridge P.
Oxalis	" "	Willow Av. and round the upper half of Auburn Lake.
Peony	" "	Chapel to Cypress Av.
Petunia	" "	Larch to Magnolia Av.
Pilgrim	" "	Walnut Av. to Snowdrop P.
Primrose	" "	Central to Culvert Av.
Pyrola	" "	Spruce Av. to Orange P.
Rhodora	" "	Oak to Larch Av.
Rose	encircles	Harvard Hill.
Rosemary	leads from	Jasmine to Hawthorn P.
Saffron	" "	Spruce Av. to St. John's Lot.
Sedge	" "	Fir Av. to Heath P.
Sorrel	" "	Spruce to Fir Av.
Snowberry	" "	Pine near the Gate to Central Av.
Snowdrop	" "	Walnut to Spruce Av.
Spiræa	" "	Fir Av. to Mistletoe P.
Sumac	" "	Moss to Violet P. and Walnut Av.
Sweet Brier	" "	Chestnut Av. to Hawthorn P.
Sylvan	" "	Walnut to Mountain Av.
Thistle	" "	Spruce Av. to Cowslip P.
Trefoil	" "	Spruce to Walnut Av.
Tulip	" "	Walnut Av. to Trefoil P.
Verbena	" "	Spruce to Fir Av.
Vine	" "	Moss to Iris P.
Woodbine	" "	Hawthorn to Ivy P.
Yarrow	" "	Green Brier, westerly to Fir Av., thence easterly to Pine Av.

Hazel Dell, between Central Avenue and Indian Ridge Path.
Consecration Dell, the deep hollow north of the Tower.
Central Square, between Walnut Avenue and Moss and Ivy Paths.

INDEX.

www.ingramcontent.com/pod-product-compliance
Lightning Source LLC
LaVergne TN
LVHW011941060326
832903LV00045B/112